CHERISHED

LIBRARY
BOOK HOUSE
BRIGHTON

Gabriel N Cherish

BRIGHTON
A Very
Peculiar
History

With added Hove, actually

'The people are very indiscreet and troublesome here really, which makes the place quite like a prison.'
Queen Victoria

Editor: Stephen Haynes
Additional artwork: David Antram,
Mark Bergin, John James,
Nick Hewetson, Rob Walker

Published in Great Britain in MMIX by
Book House, an imprint of
The Salariya Book Company Ltd
25 Marlborough Place, Brighton BN1 1UB
www.salariya.com
www.book-house.co.uk

HB ISBN-13: 978-1-906714-89-5

© The Salariya Book Company Ltd MMIX
All rights reserved. No part of this publication may be reproduced, stored in or
introduced into a retrieval system or transmitted in any form, or by any means
(electronic, mechanical, photocopying, recording or otherwise) without the written
permission of the publisher. Any person who does any unauthorised act in relation to this
publication may be liable to criminal prosecution and civil claims for damages.

5 7 9 8 6
A CIP catalogue record for this book is available
from the British Library.
Printed and bound in China.
Printed on paper from sustainable sources.
Reprinted in MMXIV.

This book is sold subject to the conditions that it shall not, by way of trade or
otherwise, be lent, resold, hired out, or otherwise circulated without the publisher's
prior consent in any form or binding or cover other than that in which it is published
and without similar condition being imposed on the subsequent purchaser.

Visit our website at **www.book-house.co.uk**
or go to **www.salariya.com**
for **free** electronic versions of:
You Wouldn't Want to be an Egyptian Mummy!
You Wouldn't Want to be a Roman Gladiator!
You Wouldnt Want to Join Shackleton's Polar Expedition!
You Wouldn't Want to Sail on a 19th-Century Whaling Ship!

Visit
www.salariya.com
for our online catalogue and
free interactive web books.

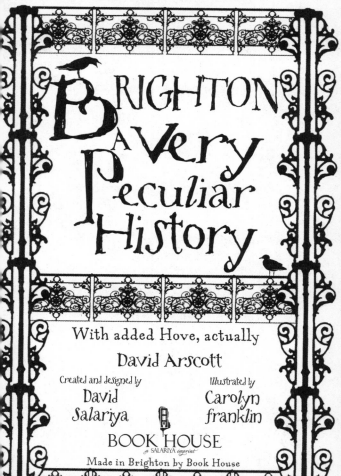

BRIGHTON
A Very Peculiar History

With added Hove, actually

David Arscott

Created and designed by
David Salariya

Illustrated by
Carolyn Franklin

BOOK HOUSE
a SALARIYA imprint

Made in Brighton by Book House

'A visit to Brighton comprised every possibility of earthly happiness.'
Jane Austen, *Pride and Prejudice*

'It is the fashion to run down George IV, but what myriads of Londoners ought to thank him for inventing Brighton! One of the best of physicians our city has ever known, is kind, cheerful, merry Doctor Brighton.
W. M. Thackeray, *The Newcomes*

'Brighton looks like a town that is constantly helping the police with their enquiries.'
Keith Waterhouse

'Anyone who does not live in Brighton must be mad and ought to be locked up.'
S. P. B. Mais

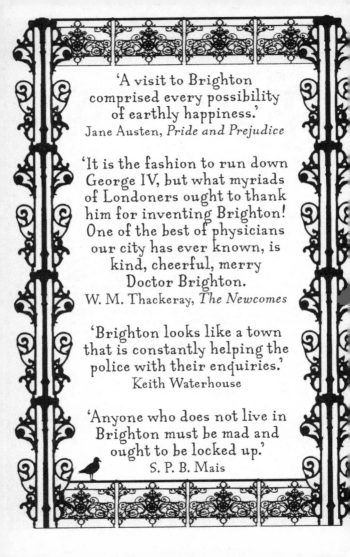

Contents

Ten places that Brighton *isn't*

1. **Eastbourne.** A resort a little to the east of Brighton 'built *by* gentlemen *for* gentlemen'. It still has the reputation of being comfortably genteel and elderly – whereas Brighton is young and exciting.

2. **Littlehampton.** West of Brighton, deserted for much of the year and with a vast expanse of sand. Brighton is always busy – and, except at low tide, its seafront is deep in lovely shingle.

3. **Blackpool.** Up in the chilly north-west, with three piers, a famous tower and crowds of noisy people eating fish & chips and whelks, although not necessarily at the same time. Two of Brighton's three piers have gone and it has no tower as yet – but it's warmer here, and the visitors are much more cultured.

4. **Scarborough.** Up in the chilly north-east, miles from anywhere and with a cliff that is dramatically collapsing into the sea. It's warmer in Brighton – and the cliff fell into the sea centuries ago.

5. **Torremolinos.** A haven for badly dressed tourists getting drunk and singing the Chicken Song. Brighton's cooler – and some of us prefer Glyndebourne opera house for our music.

6. **Robinson Crusoe's island.** Hot, uninhabited, sprinkled with palm trees and serenely peaceful – but can you imagine the boredom?

7. **Rotterdam.** Europe's largest port, and a fine example of how to turn an area of coast into a bustling commercial centre, with industries packed along the quaysides. There's little sign of heavy industry in Brighton, thankfully – although the occasional fishing boat bobs by.

8. **Rio de Janeiro.** The home of the body beautiful, with sun-tanned strutters parading the beach to a backdrop of Sugarloaf Mountain. Brighton has its own nudist beach, the very first officially designated one in Britain – but you really wouldn't want to witness the shivering humanity who perch their naked bottoms on the unforgiving Brighton pebbles.

9. **London.** No, of course not – but Brighton has long been known as London-by-the-Sea because of the vast numbers of people who flock in from the capital whenever they get the chance – and they know a good thing when they see it.

10. **Paris.** No, again, but we're getting warmer. The French capital has a reputation not only for elegant good living, but also for being rather 'naughty'. Think of Brighton as Paris with the sea tacked on.

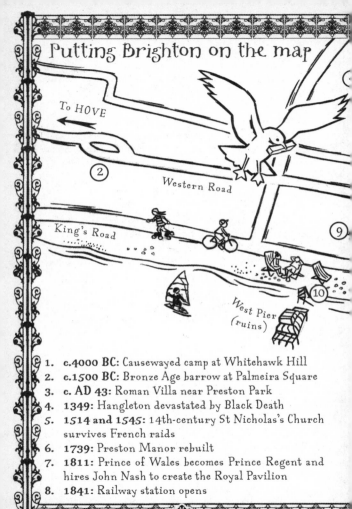

Putting Brighton on the map

To HOVE

Western Road

King's Road

West Pier (ruins)

1. **c.4000 BC:** Causewayed camp at Whitehawk Hill
2. **c.1500 BC:** Bronze Age barrow at Palmeira Square
3. **c. AD 43:** Roman Villa near Preston Park
4. **1349:** Hangleton devastated by Black Death
5. **1514 and 1545:** 14th-century St Nicholas's Church survives French raids
6. **1739:** Preston Manor rebuilt
7. **1811:** Prince of Wales becomes Prince Regent and hires John Nash to create the Royal Pavilion
8. **1841:** Railway station opens

9. **1984:** Grand Hotel damaged by IRA bomb
10. **2009:** Plans to build a high-tech observation tower at the land end of the ruined West Pier are said to be well advanced

Hove, actually

- Until the two boroughs were officially merged in 1997, Brighton and Hove were uneasy neighbours with different histories who didn't quite get on.

- As far as Hove was concerned, young Brighton was noisy, boisterous, chippy – a bit too full of itself.

- Brighton thought Hove was dull, elderly and unimaginative – something of a drag.

- Attitudes such as these don't change overnight. The Peace Statue on the seafront marks the dividing line between the two, and local inhabitants are acutely aware of which side they live on.

- Suggest to someone west of the boundary that they come from Brighton, and the stock response is, 'Hove, actually'.

- You hear it so often that it's almost become part of the address.

INTRODUCTION

What makes Brighton special?

We all love the seaside and the sense of freedom it brings, but Brighton has a reputation above all other resorts in Britain for the 'edgy' pleasures it offers to visitors from all over the world.

It's not a bucket-and-spade kind of place, but a sophisticated 'melting pot' for a wide variety of people who relish the idea of having a good time in their own way.

In fact (and don't you dare tell them this), sometimes it feels like a place for grown-ups who haven't quite grown up at all.

The observant reader will already have noticed that the early chapters of this book are fairly short. That's not just because it took a long time for a proper town to develop here (as we shall see, it first became prosperous in medieval times), but because Brighton discovered its true purpose in life only about 250 years ago.

That purpose has been to attract visitors in their droves, parting them from their cash – and sometimes from their common sense, too – in return for an endless, and colourfully varied, range of entertainments.

Of course, the people who live here care very much about things like schools, hospitals and rubbish collections, but that's certainly not what Brighton means to everyone else. As far as the wider world is concerned it isn't really owned by its inhabitants at all – or not in the way that matters.

It's always been a place for other people to pass through on their way to somewhere else, or to pause in for a little fun before going away again. This has given it a very peculiar history.

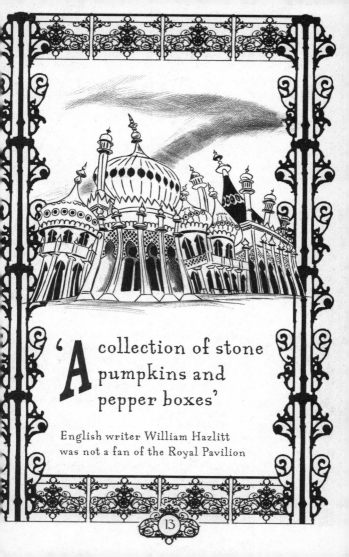

'A collection of stone pumpkins and pepper boxes'

English writer William Hazlitt was not a fan of the Royal Pavilion

The obsession with having a good time began with George, the Prince Regent, and his extravagant friends (can you imagine the gaudy Royal Pavilion being built in any other seaside town?), and it hasn't stopped since.

In many ways this has been very useful for Brighton. The rich folk who came here during the 18th century for the 'sea-water cure' helped to revive a town that was very much down on its luck.

What's in a name?

It wasn't until 1810 that the authorities decided officially to call their town Brighton.

Before that it was known as something like Brighthelmston, although more than 40 variations on the theme have been recorded. (In the Domesday Book it was Bristelmestune.)

The 'tun' bit signifies a homestead, and the best guess is that someone called Beorthelm (which means 'bright helmet') was the bigwig here in Saxon times – but, if so, the poor chap's been completely forgotten.

But the influx of so many outsiders can cause problems, too. Once the railway had arrived in the 1840s, Brighton grew faster than any other town in Britain, and during the later Victorian period many areas were horribly overcrowded, with foul-smelling slums that were a terrible health hazard because people drank water raised in buckets from wells that lay right next to their cesspits.

During the 1930s, day-trippers arrived here in their thousands, but some of them weren't the kind of people you'd want as next-door neighbours. There were razor-wielding gangs who frequented the racecourse, and for a time the town had a very bad reputation indeed.

Fortunately, Brighton has always found ways to rise above its problems, knowing that unless it puts on a good show for its visitors it can't hope to be prosperous.

Today, as we shall see, it's a bright and cheerful city, but – just like some of the characters who like to have their fun here – it has a colourful and occasionally disreputable past. Read on . . .

What's under your feet?

The first thing you need to know about Brighton is that the land it sits on wasn't always there.

Let's go back a hundred million years to a Sussex that wasn't the attractive jumble of hills and valleys we know today, but a flat expanse of nothing, covered by water.

At one period this was a swampy region, criss-crossed by meandering rivulets and inhabited by iguanodons and other dinosaurs. Later it was flooded by the sea. The bands of sediment that built up on the bottom hardened to become the eventual rocks and soils of Sussex: sandstones, clay, shales, limestone and chalk. During all these vast aeons they lay in an orderly fashion, one on top of the other, quietly minding their own business.

The chalk, on top of everything else, was created from minute calcite crystals secreted by planktonic algae when the land was under the sea, and it built up at the rate of a metre every 100,000 years for all of 30 million years to form layers some 300 metres thick.

So why isn't the landscape flat today? Because once, another very long time ago, there was a gradual but violent grinding of the tectonic plates (sections of the earth's crust) that lie beneath our continent.

It lifted, twisted and buckled the rocks to form the Alps in northern Europe and create the huge, if less dramatic, dome that eventually became today's Sussex. Geologists call it the Wealden anticline – and Brighton sits on the southern edge of it.

Once rivers had cut through the rocks on their way to the sea, and once rain, frost and ice had scoured and weathered the surface over millions more years, Sussex was left with the broad bands of soils which make up our Downs and Weald today.[1]

Don't imagine, though, that the beach we walk the dog on today is where the earliest inhabitants of Sussex found it half a million years ago. The fickle sea was sometimes 40 metres higher than it is now, and sometimes all of 100 metres lower. In the cliffs at Black Rock, near Brighton Marina, you can see evidence of an ancient beach 8 metres above the current sea level and dating from about 200,000 years ago.

It wasn't until 5,000 years ago that the sea arrived at something like the present coastline, and another 2,000 years before it reached roughly the height we know today – although it has kept ebbing and flowing ever since, and at present threatens to wash away houses all around the south-east coast of England.

1. *You might think that our chalk slopes should be called the Ups rather than the Downs, but the word comes from the Old English* dun, *which means 'hill'.*

17

Roger may not have been the sharpest flint in prehistoric Sussex.

fROM PREHISTORY TO 1066

L et's introduce you to a man called Roger. He's very old – probably half a million years old – but unfortunately we can only guess what he looked like. That's because all that remains of him is a single fragment of shin-bone.

The archaeologists who affectionately gave him his daft name (no, *of course* nobody was called Roger then) were exploring an ancient raised beach at Boxgrove, 32 km (20 miles) west of Brighton, near Chichester. They also found a couple of teeth, but these probably belonged to someone else.

• Early Stone Age/Palaeolithic era (to 8000 BC)

The Boxgrove people were members of a species we know as *Homo heidelbergensis* – their descendants being Neanderthal man (now extinct) and possibly ourselves (not yet) – and they lived in a climate similar to our own. They collected flints from the base of the cliffs and chipped away at them to fashion razor-sharp hand-axes. With these they hunted and butchered rhinoceroses, bears, bison, horses and large deer.

But there were chilly times to come. Some 14,000 years ago, with glaciers forming further north, the Downs were covered by snowfields and the chalk was permanently frozen. The snow melted when the last ice age ended, and rivers cut through the hills, scouring out the valley north of Brighton which we know as Devil's Dyke (see page 23).

• Middle Stone Age/Mesolithic (8000–4300 BC)

As the temperature rose, life became easier for the nomadic hunter-gatherers and hunter-fishers who foraged along the coast and in the dense oak forests of Sussex, which teemed with wild cattle, deer and pigs.

Their rock-shelters have been excavated in the Sussex Weald, especially on the high ground to the north of Brighton, but scatterings of their worked flints have been found in the Brighton area, too.

• New Stone Age/Neolithic (4300–1500 BC)

Come the New Stone Age, Brighton at last finds a definite place on the prehistoric map. During this period settlers used polished stone tools, domesticated animals, practised weaving, made pottery and sank flint mines deep into the chalk – walk on the Downs above the Long Man of Wilmington chalk figure to the east of Brighton, and the indentations you see in the turf are the tops of those ancient mineshafts.

These settlers also left permanent marks on the landscape in the form of long and oval 'barrows', or burial mounds, and a series of large 'causewayed camps' on high points of the Downs. One of these camps can still be seen – although it's been knocked about more than a bit – 130 metres above sea level, up by Brighton Racecourse at Whitehawk Hill. Probably built between 4000 and 3000 BC, and extended over several centuries, it comprises four concentric earthworks with crossing points, or causeways, over the ditches.

Nobody really knows what these structures were for. They weren't sufficiently protected to have been fortifications, and the best guess is that they were centres for communal rituals of some sort.

Building a causewayed camp

The legend of Devil's Dyke

If you've seen that huge crease in the Downs above Brighton known as Devil's Dyke, you've perhaps wondered how it got there.

Old Scratch (or the Devil to you and me) had a cunning plan to drown all the little churches of the Sussex Downs in a single night. He dug a vast trench so that the sea would come in and flood them.

But why didn't he succeed? Because his frantic digging woke up a little old woman, who quickly saw what he was about. So she set a candle in her window and put a sieve in front of it to create a glowing globe. When Old Scratch saw it, he thought it must be the rising sun.

Of course he was unable to work after sunrise, so he had to give up then and there. You can still see the spoil heaps from his work standing out against the sky – Chanctonbury Ring, Cissbury Ring and Mount Caburn above Lewes.

• Bronze Age (1500–700 BC)

By 1500 BC the Bronze Age was in full swing, and the immigrant 'Beaker folk' who now extensively farmed the gentler, sea-facing slopes of the Downs have left considerable evidence of their lifestyle behind them – quite apart from the decorated, flat-bottomed storage jars and cremation urns which have given them their name.

Most of their round barrows littered the hills, but one of them (4 metres high and 30 metres in diameter) was constructed down on the coast. It was demolished in 1856 to allow the development of Palmeira Avenue in Hove.

An oak coffin was found some 3 metres below the surface, and among the grave goods were a bronze dagger, a stone axe and – most handsome of all – a cup fashioned from a single piece of red amber (now in Hove Museum). Since amber comes from the Baltic, this tells us that these people were on a trade route which brought precious goods from many hundreds of miles away. It also suggests that this was a society in which some families and individuals had grown to be very important.

• Iron Age (700 BC – AD 43)

But change was on its way. Celtic people now crossed the Channel, bringing with them the skill of smelting and forging iron.

Look up to the Downs from below and you'll see many traces of the Iron Age in Sussex, including ancient trackways still in use by walkers today. Their stronger ploughs extended arable (crop) farming, and their 'strip lynchets', or stepped fields, can sometimes be made out on the dip slopes.

Across the folds of the hills they constructed at least 60 banks known as 'cross-ridge dykes' – we don't know what they were for – and many of these are close to the hill-forts which also sprang up at this time.

Brighton is encircled by these well-defended earthworks, including the ones at Devil's Dyke and Hollingbury. Originally they must have been topped by sturdy timber palisades, and it would have been very difficult for an invading army to fight its way over the deep ditches and through the sinuous entrances.

Julius Caesar managed to seize a fort of this kind in neighbouring Kent when he came on summer raiding trips in 55 and 54 BC. But when the real Roman invasion of Sussex took place nearly a hundred years later, nobody tried to stop it at all!

• Roman Sussex (AD 43–410)

The Celtic tribes of Britain were always fighting among themselves, but the one that ruled most of Sussex had the luck to be on good terms with the mighty Roman Empire, which stretched all the way from Italy to Gaul

History – or bunk?

When we talk about 'prehistory' we're referring to those vast periods of time during which nothing was written down.

The historical period began in Sussex (and Brighton) when the Romans arrived, because they were a highly literate people who left written evidence behind them.

But that certainly doesn't mean you have to believe everything you read in ancient accounts. Ask *why* they wrote it – and always take it with a healthy pinch of salt!

26

(roughly speaking, France and Belgium) on the other side of the Channel.

Not surprisingly, therefore, when Emperor Claudius decided to invade Britain in AD 43, he was given a warm welcome here. The Second Augusta legion under Vespasian (later to become emperor himself) established a garrison at a site that would soon develop into Chichester, and Sussex became a base from which to attack the hostile tribes in the west.

The local leader, Togidubnus, was created a 'client king' by the Romans, and the great palace at Fishbourne, near Chichester, was almost certainly his reward for making their life much easier than it would otherwise have been. It was as big and possibly as sumptuous as Nero's fabulous Golden House in Rome.

We all know about the straight roads the Romans drove through the landscape (there were three major ones running down from London into Sussex), but they also built a network of smaller ones linking the villas that sprang up all over the Downs and along the coastal strip. This was fertile farming country.

Brighton's hidden river

Not many people know that a river called the Wellesbourne used to run down to the sea at Brighton, more or less following the course of the present-day London Road.

It was never much more than a stream for most of the year, but it became a bit more impressive at times of high rainfall and it sometimes caused serious flooding where it met the sea around Pool Valley (where the coach station is now).

In Roman times, it's thought that there was a small port here, its remains now probably buried out on the seabed somewhere south of the Palace Pier.

During the 1790s, when the soggy area known as the Old Steine was unattractive to the gentry, The Prince of Wales and the Duke of Marlborough paid for a wooden sewer to carry the water away underground – but that didn't solve the problem altogether.

Flooding continued every few years until the Patcham Waterworks was installed in 1889. It pumps the water away – and now the little Wellesbourne is seen no more.

There was at least one of those villas in the Brighton area, dating from the period soon after the invasion. It was discovered in 1876, close to Preston Park, and it now has a block of flats built over it. The villa seems to have been built in two stages. It had geometric black and white mosaic floors, and in its grounds there were wells lined with chalk blocks. In and around the villa, archaeologists found:

- skulls
- burial urns
- pottery fragments
- coins
- bronze tweezers
- a pin made of bone
- oyster shells
- figurines
- an iron lamp

The Romans were in charge for a long time, but that doesn't mean that the locals were bossed around by sharply dressed Italians. Under compliant native leaders like Togidubnus, ordinary people were probably left to get on with their lives much as before – although many of them would have found themselves a bit more prosperous.

But trouble was brewing. From the late third century, Saxon pirates began to carry out murderous raids along the coast. A great fort was built at Pevensey, to the east of Brighton, to keep them at bay, while nippy scout-ships, painted green and manned by crews of rowers dressed in the same colour, patrolled offshore to report on their movements.

These measures were reasonably successful, but the Roman Empire was crumbling. More and more of its soldiers were withdrawn from Britain to deal with problems closer to home until, in AD 410, the last of them packed their kitbags and left – abandoning the poor Romano-Britons to the mercy of incredibly fierce, land-hungry invaders.

They didn't show a great deal of it!

• Saxon Sussex (AD 410–1066)

Imagine the terror you'd feel if you were one of those people who suddenly found themselves unprotected in the face of these hostile invaders. Here are three of your options:

- **To be killed outright**
- **To be captured and made into a slave**
- **To escape westwards and never return home**

Unfortunately there weren't any others.

National hero?

Some wonderful stories have been told about King Arthur and his legendary Round Table (Lancelot, Guinevere and the rest), but did he really exist?

If he did, he may have been a tribal leader at the time when the Romans pulled out of Britain, helping his Celtic people to fight off the marauding Saxons.

History has no record of a single great chieftain who fits the bill, but there were probably several 'Prince Arthurs' who displayed great heroism in a losing cause – and left a powerful folk memory behind them.

Saxons go home!

Some Saxon place-names in the Brighton area

We've already seen (page 14) how Brighton got its name. Here are a few more local derivations . . .

Bevendean *Beofan dene* A dene is a valley, and it was apparently owned by a man named Beofa.

Blatchington *Blaecing tun* This was the *tun*, or farmstead, of a man whose nickname was 'the black one' – probably not someone to mess with.

Falmer *Faele mere* It means 'yellow pond' – and the pond is still here, yellow or not, more than a thousand years later.

Hangleton *Hangra tun* Farmstead on the slope – and the ground *does* fall away south of St Helen's church.

Hollingbury The *bury* bit is the Iron Age hill-fort we've already discovered, and perhaps holly was prolific here – but nobody knows how old the name is, and therefore what it means.

Hove A bit of a mystery, but etymologists (the experts in ferreting out word origins) think it may refer to a small dwelling, or 'hovel', of the kind that used to be erected by the wayside for the comfort of passing travellers. Present-day residents may be none too happy with this explanation.

Moulsecoomb *Muls cumb* The man who ran the show in this 'coombe', or valley, was perhaps an obstinate character, because 'Mul' was a nickname meaning 'mule'.

Ovingdean *Ofinga dene* The valley owned by a tribe known as the Ofingas, probably with a leader named Ofa.

Patcham *Piceham* The settlement, or *ham*, of a man called Pecca.

Portslade *Portes lad* This was the crossing (*gelad*) of the port, which suggests that the mouth of the River Adur was once some way further east than it is today.

Preston (Village) *Preosta tun* The farmstead of the priests. It once belonged to the Bishop of Chichester.

Rottingdean *Rotinga dene* Like Ovingdean: the valley of the Rotingas, or Rota's people.

Stanmer *Stan mere* Another pond, and this time a stony one. The name's recorded like this as early as AD 765, and the pond doesn't seem to have changed much since.

Whitehawk Nobody knows!

Withdean By now you'll have guessed that this was a valley lorded over by a Saxon character named something like 'With'. Close: he's thought to have been called Wihta.

Once they had settled here, the Saxons set about creating the Sussex we know today. Our village names are practically all Saxon in origin, and many of our parish boundaries, too. After St Wilfrid converted the people to Christianity in AD 681, wooden churches were built all over the landscape, and many of the sites that were chosen are still occupied today by the stone buildings that succeeded them.

There were momentous events and great changes during this 600-year period. Viking invaders were driven off by King Alfred, who built a chain of *burhs*, or forts, in Sussex – one of them at nearby Lewes, which had become a thriving town, with a mint to produce coins. By now the kingdom of the South Saxons (what we call 'Sussex') had grown pretty prosperous.

So, when did Beorthelm make his mark in what we know as Brighton? We just don't know. All we can say with any confidence is that in the late Saxon period there was some kind of village here – and we know *that* only because of what happened after a certain battle in 1066, some 56 km (35 miles) to the north-east.

CHAPTER TWO

MEDIEVAL BRIGHTON'S RISE AND FALL

It was Norman invader William the Conqueror who first put little Brighton on the map. Soon after the Battle of Hastings in 1066, he sent his commissioners all over the country to record who owned the land and how much it was worth for tax purposes. As you can imagine, this didn't make them very popular visitors. But they wrote up their findings in the Domesday Book, one of the most valuable documents in English history.

What we know from the Domesday Book is that Brighton was a small fishing village, perhaps with not many more than a hundred inhabitants, and that it had a church – no doubt a wooden one, and probably on a site which is now somewhere out to sea. It's thought that the settlement was on a broad chalk foreshore beneath low cliffs, with some farming on the Downs above. Among the residents was a single slave – perhaps a descendant of the Celts whom the Saxons had thrown out all those centuries before. He had a new master now.

At the time of the Conquest the manor was owned by Brictric, but the Normans promptly turfed out all the Saxon lords (400 of them throughout Sussex) and handed everything over to their own people – the lucky man in this case, Domesday tells us, being Ralph.

The manor of Brighton was valued at £12. That figure by itself is meaningless today, but it's useful for making comparisons with other villages (see page 38). The locals had to pay Ralph an annual rent of 4,000 herrings. That may sound a lot, but nearby Southease – which is only a hamlet on the River Ouse nowadays – had to hand over all of 38,500 herrings, plus £4 'for porpoises' and three packloads of peas.

We're doomed!
A taxing time for Bristelmestune.

Lewes, upriver from Southease, was at that time a thriving port and the largest of only seven towns in the whole of Sussex. When you consider that the population of the entire county was only about 60,000, you realise how small many of these places were. As for Hove, it may have just about existed, but it wasn't significant enough to get even the smallest mention in the Domesday Book.

A few other local places in the Domesday Book

Aldrington 51 villagers, 22 smallholders. 'There is only one hall.' Worth £11.

Bevendean Two villagers, three smallholders. Worth £6.

Falmer A church, 35 villagers, seven smallholders, one slave, 20 pigs. Worth £20.

Hangleton 31 villagers, 13 smallholders. Worth £10.

Ovingdean 'A small church', five villagers, five smallholders, four slaves. Worth £7.

Patcham A church, 168 villagers, 45 smallholders, six slaves, ten shepherds and 100 pigs. Worth £80.

Portslade Two villagers. Worth 12 shillings (just 60p).

Preston A church, a mill, 39 villagers, 23 smallholders. Worth £18.

Rottingdean Ten smallholders. Worth £3.

Stanmer 49 villagers, 10 smallholders and six pigs. Worth £15.

and Hove? Actually, it's not even mentioned!

Growing Bigger

Edward II granted Brighton a market charter[1] and fair in 1313 – a sure sign that it was becoming a relatively busy trading centre – and it grew slowly but steadily over the next few centuries.

While the fishermen kept their boats under the cliff, the rest of the town developed on higher ground above. In 1185 we first find mention of a chapel and priory dedicated to St Bartholomew, on the site of today's Town Hall, but the parish church of St Nicholas probably already existed then, looking down on the rectangle of little streets we now know as the Old Town.

Despite a steady 'infilling' of new houses as the town's population increased, this was the extent of Brighton even as late as the 1750s: a compact area between North Street, West Street, East Street and the sea, with the church up on its hill to the north-west.

1. *Permission from the King to hold a market in the town. Brighton's marketplace was near the site of the present Town Hall.*

Lanes and *laines*

Some people get in a terrible muddle about what to call two very different shopping areas in Brighton. Get this right and you'll show that you really know what's what.

The Lanes are the little alleyways (called 'twittens' in Sussex) in the oldest part of Brighton – bordered by North Street, East Street, Ship Street and the Town Hall area. In the early days this was a humble fishermen's quarter called Hempshares, where hemp was either grown or twisted into rope. Today it's the home of jewellers, antique shops and other fashionable outlets – the Queen paid a visit on the day she opened the Marina in 1979.

Laines were five open medieval fields on the downland around Brighton: West Laine, North Laine, Hilly Laine, Little Laine and East Laine. They were divided into 'furlongs', separated from one another by paths known as 'leakways'. When the town spread outwards in the 18th and 19th centuries, these paths became major east–west roads across the town, such as Western Road and St James's Street.

The **North Laine** (below the railway station and several blocks north of the Lanes) is now an exciting, offbeat area packed with wacky one-off shops. Don't make the mistake of calling this area the 'North Laines' (plural), or you'll show everyone that you're a 'furriner'!

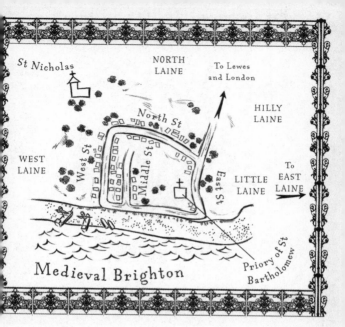

Medieval Brighton

Catching and selling fish was what first made Brighton prosperous, and the 'jugs' (as the local fishermen were called) were a resourceful lot.

Hauling boats onto the beach wasn't an easy business, even with the help of horses, so they developed a shallow type of boat known as a 'hoggie' – although they called it a 'hogboat' when they were on their best behaviour.

A Brighton 'hoggie'

It was broad in the beam so that it wouldn't capsize easily, it had triangular lee-boards hung on the sides to avoid being blown to windward, and it's been described – rather unkindly – as 'a small, round little tub'.

With their fleet of trusty hoggies, the jugs not only fished off the Sussex coast (and ran other cargoes up local rivers as a sideline) but caught mackerel and herring in the English Channel and sailed as far as the North Sea. They caught herring off Yarmouth in Norfolk from September to November, and cod off Scarborough in Yorkshire between June and

September. The men would be away from home for months at a time.

A 'Book of Auncient Customs' records that in 1580 there were 400 fishermen in Brighton, with 80 boats and 10,000 nets. They worked as a co-operative: all had shares in the catch, with a percentage also going towards the town's defences and the maintenance of the church.

By 1650, while Hove was still little more than a row of cottages in Hove Street, Brighton had become the largest town in Sussex, with a population of around 4,000.

Troubled times

Just in case you think this was an unbroken success story, with never a cloud on the horizon, we should point out a few unfortunate events that the locals had to survive . . .

• **The Black Death**
Between a quarter and a third of the English population died after bubonic plague entered the country in 1349. We don't know how it

affected Brighton itself, but next door in Hangleton it caused devastation.

Before the Black Death arrived, the village had a population of around 200, and the people were already suffering from several years of poor harvests and disease among their sheep and cattle. Now, it's thought, up to 60 per cent of them perished in a most horrible way – in a delirium and vomiting blood. By 1428 there were only two households left.

Before the Black Death

13th-century cottage from Hangleton, reconstructed at the Weald and Downland Open-Air Museum, near Chichester, West Sussex

St Helen's church stood alone as a reminder of happier times until, in the 1540s, Richard Bellingham used stone from Lewes Priory (dismantled on the orders of Henry VIII) to build Hangleton Manor. It's now the oldest domestic building in all of Brighton and Hove.

• French pirates

This sounds very jolly, but the reality was much more frightening. We needn't go into the so-called Hundred Years' War with France – which actually lasted from 1337 until 1453, with a few 'comfort breaks' in between. Suffice to say that the Sussex coast was bedevilled over a very long period by murderous raiders who burned whole towns to the ground, stole what they could and did other unspeakable things while they were about it.

Oh, and let's confess that some of our people did much the same on the other side of the Channel, too. Brighton fishermen were among those who not only raided the coastal parts of France, but attacked French ships and smuggled contraband goods into the country on a large scale.

Brighton sacked by the French

In 1377 the villagers of nearby Rottingdean retreated into St Margaret's church when pirates set fire to their houses, only to find that the church itself was burning.

Brighton itself was viciously sacked in 1514 and 1545. A drawing in the British Museum shows several houses on fire, with 13 warships off shore and a number of galleys on the beach. The 1545 raid followed an unsuccessful French attack on Portsmouth and the Isle of Wight which brought about the capsizing of Henry VIII's flagship, the *Mary Rose*.

A brave brewer

During the reign of the Roman Catholic queen 'Bloody Mary' (1553–1558), dozens of Protestants were burned at the stake in Lewes. The first was Derrick Carver, a Flemish brewer who had set up his business in Black Lion Street, Brighton. (Today there's a plaque on the wall.)

At his trial he told the bishop defiantly: 'You say that you can make a God. Ye can make a pudding as well.' As the flames licked around him, he threw his Bible into the watching crowd in an attempt to save it.

After these raids the people of Brighton had to rebuild their town – only St Nicholas's church, on its hill outside the Old Town, survives from the earlier period. They built a defensive wall and a 'blockhouse' on the seafront. This was a circular fort with walls 2.4 metres (8 ft) thick, topped by six large guns and ten small ones.

• The Armada

They might have needed it! As if the French weren't enough, along came the vast Spanish fleet, intent on the overthrow of the Protestant Queen Elizabeth.

The Armada was first sighted off Selsey in West Sussex on 25 July 1588, but the warning beacons had been fired across the land days before. The nation held its breath.

The two deputy lieutenants for the county, Sir Thomas Palmer and Walter Coverte, had the previous year been instructed to make a survey of the coast to determine how vulnerable it was to invasion. The news wasn't good for local people: the coastline from Shoreham to 'Brighthempston' allowed easy landing, 'for defence wherof yt were necessarie that ii Dimiculverings [two medium-sized cannon] and ii Sacres [two smaller ones] were kept in some good howse to be redie at sudden'.

Whether these specific guns were in place in time we don't know, but the blockhouse on the seafront was given more cannon, and a barrel of gunpowder was sent down from Lewes.

Mercifully, not a shot needed to be fired. The great Armada sailed slowly past, with English ships in hot pursuit – and within days it was in ruins, with only 44 of the original 130 warships able to limp back home.

Thank your lucky stones

If you're the superstitious type, you may like to hunt along the foreshore in the Brighton area to bring yourself some good fortune.

Fossilised sea-urchins, otherwise known as shepherds' crowns and thunder stones, have long been regarded as lucky charms. They've even been found in Neolithic, Bronze Age and Iron Age graves, presumably to give their owners a better chance in the afterlife.

Much more common are beach stones with holes in them. The people of Sussex used to wear these 'hag stones' on strings around their necks to ward off witches and other evils, and fishermen would never go to sea without a collection of them on their boats.

But you don't have to *keep* them. One tradition still remembered by older folk was to spit through the hole and then throw the stone over your left shoulder. Do look behind you first!

The Great Escape

You may have heard a far-fetched story about the future King Charles II hiding in an oak tree after the Battle of Worcester in 1651 – the last battle of the English Civil War. This was less than three years after his father, Charles I, had been beheaded, and young Charles was now threatened with the same grisly fate himself.

Forget the oak tree, which we can't confirm. The story that follows is completely true – and even better:

Once he knew the battle was lost, Charles went into disguise. He shaved off his dark locks, 'dressed down' to look like a servant, and called himself Will Jackson.

There was only one way to survive – to pass undetected through counties bristling with Roundhead troops and find a ship that would take him across the Channel to safety.

One of his companions was Colonel George Gounter (or Gunter) of Racton House in West Sussex. We know exactly what happened because Gounter's account of the daring escape was found in the secret drawer of an old bureau when the house was dismantled in the 1830s.

Gounter had no naval contacts, but he spun a yarn to a Chichester merchant he knew about a couple of friends who were in trouble because of a duel and needed to get out of the country in a hurry. The merchant promised to help.

With another royalist sympathiser, Lord Wilmot,[1] Gounter accompanied 'Will Jackson' on horseback from Wiltshire, where he was in hiding, through Hampshire and into Sussex. They had some nasty scares near the river crossings at Arundel and Bramber before arriving, on the night of 14 October, in Brighton.

Here, at the George Inn, West Street, they were introduced to Nicholas Tettersell, whose coal brig, *The Surprise*, lay at anchor near Shoreham. Tettersell, a canny man, realised the identity of his passenger and demanded an extra fee as insurance for his boat. They sailed at two o'clock the next morning.

After Charles came home to reclaim the crown in 1660, Tettersell was so well rewarded that he was able to buy the Old Ship Inn on the seafront.

His memorial in St Nicholas's churchyard includes the lines:

> *When Charles ye Greate was nothing*
> *but a breath*
> *This valiant soule stept between him*
> *and death.*

---

1. *Father of John Wilmot, Earl of Rochester, the notorious poet.*

A large step backwards

Alas, having survived all these tribulations to become the most prosperous town in Sussex, Brighton now slipped into a sorry decline.

The sea was largely to blame. In the space of just a few generations, violent storms not only eroded the cliff (the blockhouse began to crumble), but washed the foreshore away – which meant that the fishermen had nowhere to beach and repair their boats.

The writer Daniel Defoe recorded that the ferocious storm of 1703 'stript a great many houses, turn'd up the lead of the church, overthrew two windmills, and laid them flat on the ground, the town in general (at the approach of daylight) looking as though it had been bombarded.' He also thought that the cost of installing groynes to protect the beach was more than the whole town was worth!

To add to Brighton's woes, French ships and Spanish-controlled 'Dunkirker' pirate ships were once again causing trouble by seizing English boats; there was a drop in demand for fish across Europe; and Yarmouth decided to impose restrictions on fishermen coming into its territory from outside the area.

The Brighton jugs tried to make up for this by increasing their local coastal trade, but it wasn't nearly successful enough to make up the difference. After all, there was no natural harbour here: Lewes on the River Ouse and Shoreham on the Adur enjoyed much better access to the area north of Brighton.

By the 1740s the outlook was grim:

• The population had shrunk by half from its 1650 peak – to around 2,000 – and many of its humble houses stood empty.

• There were about 450 households in the town, but three-quarters of them were excused paying rates because they were so poor.

• Indeed, because so many of them were unemployed, other parts of the country had to pay a rate to support them.

Something had to be done about it!

 I'll say!

A Druids' stone?

What's a huge 20-tonne rock doing in the south-west corner of Hove Park?

A sign next to it tells us that it's 'The Tolmen or Holy Stone of Druids', but that's probably just someone's fanciful idea.

What we do know is that it originally lay not far away, on farmland at Goldstone Bottom. In Victorian times the farmer got so fed up with sightseers trampling his crops that he sank a large hole and buried it. But the memory of it never went away, and more than half a century later it was dug up and moved here.

Brighton & Hove Albion used to play across the road at the Goldstone football ground, itself now buried under a large retail 'park'.

Some people have claimed to see the outline of a human face in the Goldstone, but you'll have to look very hard and use your imagination.

CHAPTER THREE

PRINNY AND ALL THAT

Can you imagine drinking a glass of sea water? Ugh! Yet the rebirth of Brighton begins with the idea that swigging it and swimming in it did you the power of good. This would supposedly:

- Get rid of tumours and 'eruptions'
- Clear your head
- Whiten your teeth
- Keep your bowels regular (sorry about that).

These notions were put forward in all seriousness by Dr Richard Russell, a Lewes medical man who sent his patients to Brighton for the 'sea water cure' and later moved to the town himself. Oh, and he also sold pills made from crabs' eyes, woodlice, snails, vipers' flesh and tar. Don't try this at home.

Russell wasn't the first person to think the seaside was healthy – people were already coming to Brighton and other places such as Margate, Weymouth and Scarborough – but in 1750 he published a book with the catchy title *A Dissertation on the Use of Seawater in the Diseases of the Glands*. In case that sounded too exciting, he wrote it in Latin, but three years later he brought out an English version and everyone began to take notice of him.

NOT a fishing village

One myth you'll read everywhere is that Brighton was transformed from 'a humble little fishing village' almost overnight. Not so!

We've already seen that it was the biggest town in Sussex, though fallen on hard times. Because of this there was plenty of spare land about, plenty of empty buildings ready to be rented out to visitors and plenty of unemployed people glad of new work to do.

Smart businessmen even bottled Brighton seawater and sold it in London as 'oceanic fluid'.

Meet 'the Fashion'

Wealthy people – otherwise known as 'the Fashion' – began to flock in from nearby Lewes, from Tunbridge Wells (where there had long been a spa dispensing foul-tasting spring water) and, of course, from London.

Within a little more than ten years Brighton had all the facilities its discerning clientele could wish for:

• Assembly room	1752
• Coffee house	1752
• Bathing machines	1754
• Library	1759
• Hot & cold baths	1769
• Theatre	1773

By 1780 Brighton had become the largest and swankiest resort in Britain, and its rapid growth had filled the compact area of the Old Town almost to bursting.

Limbs of Satan

If you wanted to take the plunge into the sea at Brighton (dressed in a long, shapeless gown), the accepted thing to do was to pay a 'dipper' to look after you.

The beaches for men and women were mixed at first, but attitudes changed and after 1800 they were carefully segregated. Here's an advertisement aimed at women:

'This is to acquaint the Nobility, Gentry and others resorting to Brighthelmston that Martha Tutt, Mary Guildford, Susannah Guildford, Elizabeth Wingham and Ann Smith, five strong Women, all used to the Sea, have completely fitted up a set of NEW MACHINES, with a Careful Man and a Horse, to conduct them in and out of the Water, for the purpose of BATHING LADIES AND CHILDREN.'

Men, of course, would have a male guardian – who was, no doubt, even stronger. After the poet and essayist Charles Lamb had braved the experience at Brighton, he referred to his tormentors with a shudder as 'limbs of Satan'.

Martha Gunn and John 'Smoaker' Miles were the most famous of the dippers:

'There's plenty of dippers and jokers
And salt-water rigs for your fun;
The King of them all is Old Smoaker,
The Queen of them all, Martha Gunn.'

Bathing machines on Brighton beach

Kill or cure! Dr Russell felt that an ice-cold dip followed by a drink of cuttlefish bones, woodlice and crabs' eyes, topped up with bicarbonate of soda, would hit all the right spots.

A busy old day

You really didn't have a minute to yourself if you were one of the Fashion. You were supposed to sign up, or 'subscribe', to various kinds of entertainment, and the whole (expensive) social round was engineered by the Master of Ceremonies. Here's a typical day, beginning at around 6.00 a.m.:

- Sea bathing, or a visit to the indoor baths
- To the coffee house to talk, write letters or read the papers
- Public breakfast at the Old Ship or the Castle (the first two hotels in Brighton)
- Church or chapel
- Afternoon: various amusements, such as riding on the Downs, visiting libraries, watching entertainments on the Steine,[1] attending public teas
- Dinner
- Evening: dress balls, cards, theatre etc.

1. The broad, flat thoroughfare running past the Royal Pavilion to the sea, which was a fashionable promenade in Regency times. It's now called the Old Steine, and its name means 'stony place'.

Hove's own spa

Unlike Brighton, Hove really WAS still a fishing village while all this excitement was happening next door, but it had its own 'spa waters' bubbling up from St Ann's Well.

A large pump room was built over them, and invalids drank the rust-coloured, iron-rich liquid in the hope of a cure.

A London doctor reported that a local shepherd used it, and 'for several years past, those ewes of his flock that have drank the water of this spring have never failed bringing two lambs.'

Perhaps that wasn't the best kind of recommendation when you come to think about it, because the spa later closed down and the pump room was replaced by the little fake wellhead you can see in St Ann's Well Gardens today.

A dipper becomes a dripper

Martha Gunn was a regular visitor to the Royal Pavilion, and the story goes that on one occasion the Prince saw her slip a slab of butter into her pocket.

Engaging her in conversation, he slowly moved towards a blazing fire, where he kept her talking until the evidence of her 'crime' became uncomfortably obvious.

Enter the Prince of Wales

George Augustus Frederick, Prince of Wales (later the Prince Regent and later still King George IV, but better known to his friends as 'Prinny'), wasn't the first royal to show an interest in Brighton, and he certainly wasn't the first to behave badly here, either.

His uncle, the Duke of Cumberland, was what used to be called a 'rake', and he set the young Prinny a pretty bad example. He drank a lot, gambled large amounts of money and often mixed with the wrong kind of women – on one occasion he had to pay vast damages to another lord for being too friendly with his wife.

Part of the duke's 'roistering' (another expressive old word) involved travelling to Lewes for the races, and after a while he and his friends had the bright idea of setting up a racecourse of their own on the Downs above Brighton – the very one we know today.

Soon afterwards, in September 1783, Prinny himself paid his first visit to Brighton, and he immediately fell in love with it.

Maria fitzherbert

Unfortunately Prinny also fell in love with Mrs Fitzherbert. The beautiful Maria had three husbands (one at a time, of course):

• **Edward Weld.** She married him when she was still in her teens, and within a year he had toppled from his horse and died.

• **Thomas Fitzherbert.** She married him three years later, but he died from a chill within another three.

• **Prinny.** They met when he was 22 and she was some six years older.

The first unfortunate thing was that she was a Roman Catholic, and the heir to the throne was only allowed to marry a Protestant.

The second unfortunate thing was that Prinny was so lovesick that he refused to do the sensible thing and find someone else. He decided that he would defy his father, King George III – whom he didn't get on with anyway – and marry Maria in secret.

Ten things worth knowing about the Prince Regent

1. Born in 1762, he was the son of George III, who became insane, so from 1811 Prinny had to be regent (acting king).

2. A terrible spendthrift, he ran up huge debts.

3. He loved the arts, and was a patron of painters, musicians and architects.

4. He loved good food, which made him grow large in the tum department (see opposite).

5. He married Maria Fitzherbert – it wasn't official, but he loved her (after his fashion).

6. He also married Caroline of Brunswick – this *was* official, and he hated her.

7. His and Caroline's only child, who would have become Queen Charlotte (in which case we would have had no Queen Victoria), died in childbirth in 1817.

8. He became King George IV in 1820 when his father died.

9. He built Brighton's exotic Royal Pavilion – and wept for joy when he first gazed upon it.

10. He died in 1830 and was succeeded by his younger brother, William IV.

Corset's on – now let's see if we can squeeze you into these breeches today, sir.

The Prince's breeches, now in Brighton Museum, have a 127 cm (50 in) waist.

You can imagine how hard it was to find a clergyman who would conduct such a dubious ceremony. They found one in a debtor's gaol in London, and he was paid handsomely for putting his name to the marriage certificate.

Rumours of what had happened quickly spread, and it had to be denied in Parliament on several occasions. In fact it was *never* admitted, and it is only in recent years that the amazing truth has emerged – that Prinny and Maria had seven children who lived with her in the village of Litlington at the foot of the Downs, 29 km (18 miles) away, and passed themselves off as the Payne family.

Brighton grows and grows

If Brighton was already a byword for seaside fashion, the patronage of the extravagant heir to the throne sent it into overdrive. This was wonderful for the locals. Fishing was now a very small part of the economy. It was much more profitable to cater for all the well-to-do people pouring into town for the 'season' – which began in June and soon stretched all the way to Christmas and beyond.

A bit of bad luck

Everyone was very excited when they heard that the heir to the throne was about to visit for the first time, and they worked hard to put on a good show for him.

The Steine was illuminated, the church bells rang, there was a fireworks display and a salute was fired from the gun battery on the seafront.

Unhappily something went wrong, and the soldier given the proud duty of lighting the fuse for the guns was killed on the spot.

Few of the Fashion owned houses in the town. They needed places to rent, and they also needed accommodation for the gaggle of servants they sent down in advance and who would wait on them hand and foot during their stay.

And apart from basic supplies from the likes of butchers, bakers and candlestick makers, they wanted the services of jewellers, gold- and silversmiths, portrait painters (such vanity!), hatters and wigmakers.

Brighton was very happy to oblige. Here are some figures to show how popular the resort had become:

Year	Population	Number of visitors
1787	3,800	2,000
1794	5,700	10,000
1811	12,000	12,000
1818	18,000	11,000

And apart from the bathing, the card playing, the horse racing, the theatre and the balls, what did these rich folk get up to during the long weeks they were here?

- Jackass races on the Steine (yes, really)
- Cricket (Prinny's pitch was on the Level, and teams played for prize money)
- Boxing matches, bear baiting and cock fighting (all in the yards of local inns)
- Stag hunting
- Yacht racing.

Tickling the royal tastebuds

The sumptuous feasts enjoyed by the Prince Regent were the work of his eccentric German cook, Louis Weltje. An ugly, untidy and arrogant man, he spoke with a heavy accent, and some said that neither he nor his wife could speak English better than a pair of elephants.

Before coming to Brighton he had created a savoury spread called Weltje's Motley Paste, which was all the rage in London. With Prinny he popularised the French style of cooking and the Russian way of serving food: several elaborate courses one at a time, rather than a massive display in the centre of the table. This was a more expensive way of doing things, but Prinny never worried about the cost.

If I move a muscle, I'll burst.

Pounding the royal flesh

Who opened the first Indian takeaway restaurant in England in 1810? Sake Dean Mahomed, that's who! (It was the Hindoostanee Coffee House in London – and it failed.)

Who was the first Indian to write a book in the English language? The very same man! (*The Travels of Dean Mahomed*.)

And who opened the first Turkish baths in this country? Same again – and in Brighton.

The son of an Indian army officer, Mahomed travelled to Ireland, where he eloped with a local girl whose parents didn't approve of him.

In Brighton he opened his 'Indian medicated vapour bath', which claimed to cure diseases and relieve rheumatic pains by a form of massage. Not only was this business a great success, but he was appointed 'shampooing surgeon' (masseur) to George IV.

George, Maria and Caroline

We left Prinny happily married to Maria, with a large family yet to come – but things got very sticky after that.

For one thing, he wasn't a faithful husband, and was soon seeing rather too much of Lady Jersey. For another, he decided that a good way to pay off some of his vast debts would be to get an increased allowance from Parliament. This meant renouncing Maria and marrying the eligible Caroline of Brunswick.

They first met in 1795, only three days before the wedding, and it was a terrible match. The Duke of Wellington described Caroline as a woman 'of indelicate manners, indifferent character and not very inviting appearance'.

As far as George was concerned, she talked too much and was smelly. He turned up drunk to the wedding.

As far as Caroline was concerned, the Prince was 'very fat and nothing like as handsome as his portrait'.

Mutiny and execution

Anyone who has read Jane Austen's *Pride and Prejudice* knows that large numbers of soldiers were camped around Brighton and Hove during the Napoleonic Wars – and that they were a great attraction to eligible young ladies for miles around.

Frightening though it was to think that the French might invade at any time, the military parades, manoeuvres on the Downs and mock battles at sea were a great spectacle for the locals and for visiting gentry.

Prinny, of course, loved them too, and after Napoleon's defeat at the Battle of Waterloo in 1815 he revelled in what he thought was his very important role in the glorious victory – though in reality he had precious little to do with it.

Defences against possible invasion had begun to sprout in Brighton from 1793, including two new gun batteries on the seafront. A small barracks built north of the Royal Pavilion, between Church Street and North Street, had a special hatch in the wall so that the soldiers could be served drinks from the King & Queen pub in Marlborough Place next door.

Although life could be glamorous for the officers who bedazzled young Lydia in Jane Austen's novel, it was pretty tough for the common soldiers – and in 1795 there was a mutiny by 400 men of the Oxfordshire Regiment who were stationed near Seaford, a few miles along the coast. Protesting about the high price of bread and other food, they looted local shops and made off with sacks of corn.

Many of the local people sided with them and cheered them on, but the ringleaders were soon rounded up, and they were eventually marched to Goldstone Bottom in Hove. Here some of them were given 300 lashes, before two more – Edward Cooke and Sam Parish – were led forward and forced to kneel by their coffins before being shot.

So it wasn't all fun and games in Georgian Brighton...

The men are revolting, sir!

Nine months later, Caroline gave birth to their daughter Charlotte, but their relationship had already completely broken down. They were soon officially separated. Three days later George made out a new will, leaving all his property to 'Maria Fitzherbert, my wife', while Caroline was to get only a shilling (five pence in today's money).

It didn't take long before George was courting Maria again, begging her to forgive him. He even threatened to commit suicide. In 1800 the Pope declared that she was George's only true wife in the eyes of God – which must have helped to persuade her.

He had a fine house built for her on the Old Steine (it belongs to the YMCA today) and here she stayed when she was in Brighton. For some years they lived happily together again – as if Caroline had never happened.

A bad day at the Abbey

By the time George was crowned king at Westminster Abbey in July 1821, he had already tried to have his 'official' marriage dissolved, but there had been 800 petitions and nearly a million signatures in Caroline's defence – it seems she was much more popular than him.

'Poor woman,' wrote Jane Austen to a friend, 'I shall support her as long as I can, because she is a woman and because I hate her husband.'

It had been made clear to Caroline that she wasn't welcome at the coronation. So what did she do?

- Send her husband a letter of congratulations and a handsome coronation mug as a present?
- Stay at home and read a book by Miss Austen?
- Hold a private Queen-making party with some friends?

No. Caroline wasn't the shy and retiring type: she was determined to make a fuss.

When she tried to force her way into the Abbey, bayonets were held under her chin and the door was slammed in her face. Within a few weeks, at the age of just 53, she was dead – poisoned, she thought, although her doctors said it was an intestinal blockage.

She was buried back home in Brunswick (Braunschweig), where her memorial reads: 'Here lies Caroline, the injured Queen of England.'

Perhaps she had a point.

True love

Prinny's second spell with Maria Fitzherbert was over some years before he was crowned king, but the two never lost a deep affection for each other through all their troubles.

Maria's memorial in the Roman Catholic church of St John the Baptist in Bristol Road, Kemp Town, shows her wearing three rings, to make the point that she was still Prinny's wife, whatever the official records showed. But did George leave any evidence of *his* devotion?

Indeed he did. When he died, at the age of 67, the Duke of Wellington found a locket on his body, while it lay in an open coffin. In it was a miniature portrait of Maria – and it was duly buried with him.

She went for a soldier

Phoebe Hessel (1713–1821) disguised herself as a man and enlisted as a soldier in order to follow her sweetheart all over Europe.

Her gravestone in St Nicholas's churchyard tells us that she served for many years in the 5th Regiment of Foot, was wounded by a bayonet in the Battle of Fontenoy (1745) and survived until the grand old age of 108.

Her long life, we read, 'commenced in the time of Queen Anne and extended to the reign of George IV, by whose munificence she received comfort and support in her latter years.'

There's a suggestion that Phoebe invented some of the colourful details about her life – but Prinny always enjoyed a character (being an outsized one himself) and he granted her a pension of half a guinea (52½p) a year for life.

King George commands and we obey,

Over the hills and far away...

The Royal Pavilion

It was his cook, Louis Weltje, who found the farmhouse on the Old Steine that was Prinny's first home in Brighton.

In 1787 he had it converted by his favourite architect, Henry Holland, into a two-storey E-shaped building called the Marine Pavilion. It had a domed saloon (several workmen were killed while putting it up) with curved wings on either side.

But George was always restless for change, and he was soon adding a couple of wings and having the interior decked out in an oriental style. He also built the Dome as his stables and indoor riding school, and had a connecting tunnel (it's still there) running underground between the Dome and the Pavilion.

And then, when he became Prince Regent in 1811, George launched his grand plan for the architect John Nash to completely transform the building into a new royal palace in Bath stone and stuccoed brick – the fantastic, minaretted Royal Pavilion.

The Royal Pavilion

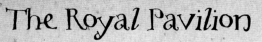

The Royal Pavilion is remarkable not only in appearance but also in construction. The architect John Nash used the most advanced technology of his day. There are huge cast-iron supports within the walls of the building to carry the weight of the cast-iron framework which supports the central dome. The tent-style roofs were covered with sheet copper.

George, the Prince of Wales, opted for an Indian-style exterior, and an interior in the Chinese style, known as 'chinoiserie'. There were many insulting comments about the Pavilion's extraordinary appearance when it was being built. The Prince was not deterred by such criticism and the Royal Pavilion became his own personal creation, a folly as extravagant as the Prince himself.

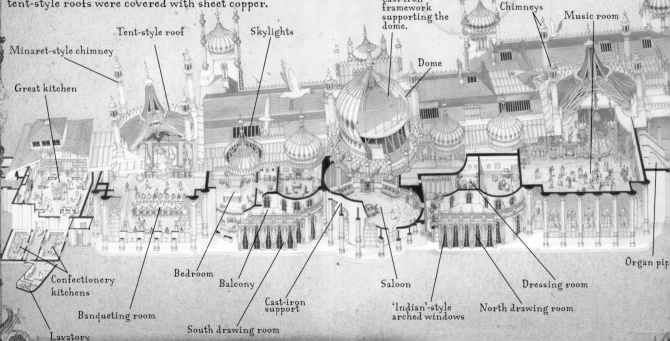

Minaret-style chimney

Great kitchen

Tent-style roof

Skylights

Cast-iron framework supporting the dome.

Chimneys

Music room

Dome

Confectionery kitchens

Banqueting room

Bedroom

Balcony

Cast-iron support

South drawing room

Saloon

'Indian'-style arched windows

Dressing room

North drawing room

Organ pip

Lavatory

George wondered
if he should have
ordered more
dragons for his gasolier.

Ten things to look out for in the Royal Pavilion

1. **Fake bamboo.** The stairs and balustrades rising from the ground floor are really made of cast iron. Even the mahogany handrails are carved with nodes to make them look like bamboo.

2. The fantastic **central chandelier (or gasolier)** in the Banqueting Room, which is 9 metres (30 feet) high and weighs one tonne (see page 79). It was originally lit by newfangled gas. There are four smaller chandeliers decorated with lotus-leaf designs.

3. The **roasting spits** above the open fire in the kitchen. These were worked by a 'smoke-jack' high up in the chimney – a sort of turbine powered by the rising heat. Prinny was very proud of his kitchen. On one occasion the famous French chef Carême (the inventor of caramel) prepared a special dinner here for Grand Duke Nicholas of Russia, with more than a hundred dishes on the menu.

4. The six huge **mirrors** in the Saloon, which create a sense of splendour in what was the King's principal reception room.

5. **Martha Gunn's portrait**, which shows her to have been a squat little person. She used to call Maria Fitzherbert 'Mrs Prince'.

6. The gorgeous **water-lily chandeliers and winged dragons** in the Music Room. The great Rossini conducted the royal band here on 20 December 1823.

7. Still in the Music Room, the **hidden door** which leads to the band room where the musicians practised.

8. More **hidden doors** in the King's bedroom – one for his valet to reach the servants' stairs, the other concealing a stairway to a private apartment above. George was overweight and suffered from gout, so didn't much like climbing stairs.

9. The entrance to the **underground passage** leading from the Pavilion to the Dome. George disliked being watched by the public, and this was his solution.

10. The Saloon **'bottle room'** (viewable only by special arrangement). The interior of the main dome above the Saloon was originally used as servants' quarters and is now covered in graffiti stretching back to the 1850s when the building was sold to Brighton Corporation by Queen Victoria.

Not everyone admired the Royal Pavilion. The writer William Cobbett said its roofscape looked like a row of upended turnips. Another critic thought St Paul's Cathedral must have had a litter of puppies on the south coast.

George was thrilled to bits with it, but he didn't enjoy its glory for long. He came down to Brighton three more times after it was finished, and then, in 1830, he died.

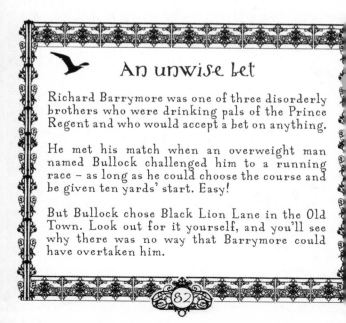

An unwise bet

Richard Barrymore was one of three disorderly brothers who were drinking pals of the Prince Regent and who would accept a bet on anything.

He met his match when an overweight man named Bullock challenged him to a running race – as long as he could choose the course and be given ten yards' start. Easy!

But Bullock chose Black Lion Lane in the Old Town. Look out for it yourself, and you'll see why there was no way that Barrymore could have overtaken him.

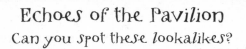

Echoes of the Pavilion

Can you spot these lookalikes?

We shall meet the architect
Amon Henry Wilds in a
moment, but here's the
house (right) he built for
himself in Western
Terrace, just off
Western Road, in 1831.
Does that dome look
familiar? Here's a clue:
he called his house the
Western Pavilion!

This building (left) behind
Eastern Terrace in Kemp
Town was created as a private
mausoleum by Sir Albert
Sassoon in 1892. His son
Edward was buried there,
too, but their remains were
removed in 1933 when the
building was sold. It was
used as an air-raid shelter
during the Second World
War, and was at one time
the Bombay Bar and
Function Room.

Regency elegance

But the Pavilion, bizarre and wonderful though it is, obviously isn't typical of Georgian Brighton as a whole.

By now Brighton was spreading out well beyond the old centre – along the coast and up into those laines on the Downs that we met in the last chapter (page 40).

It's time for some more of those exciting population statistics:

1811	12,000
1821	24,000
1831	40,000

• Two Wilds and a Busby

Three architects were responsible for most of the Regency architecture for which Brighton and Hove are famous: Amon Wilds, his son Amon Henry Wilds, and their partner Charles Augustin Busby.

Try looking around town for the Wilds' ammonites. Ammonites are fossilised sea creatures that became extinct at the same time as the dinosaurs. Their large, spiral shells are the motif used on capitals (tops of columns) by the father-and-son team as a play on the first name they shared: Amon.[1]

Ammonite capital

1. *Good places to look include Oriental Place, King's Road near the junction with East Street, Richmond Terrace, Hanover Crescent and the Montpelier area. Outside Brighton, there are two at 166 High Street, Lewes – appropriately enough, the home of the pioneer fossil-hunter Dr Gideon Mantell.*

They built a great many elegant terraces, with lovely bow-fronted windows, canopies and cast-iron balustrades (decorative railings).

To the east of the town centre they were at first beaten to it by a West Indian speculator called J. B. Otto, who built Royal Crescent (with a fine display of mathematical tiles – see opposite). It failed at the time, perhaps because it was rather isolated from the town centre, and perhaps because it had a horrible statue of George III in front of it. (Nobody knows what happened to that.)

• Kemp Town

A little later, Amon Wilds and Busby were hired by the wealthy Thomas Read Kemp to design an ambitious new estate in open country even further to the east.

Poor Kemp doesn't seem to have realised just what he was taking on. Sussex Square itself is the biggest crescent in Britain, not only larger than Grosvenor Square in London but with a diameter 60 metres (200 feet) greater than the Royal Crescent in Bath.

A bit of cheating

Regency architects loved brick and stone, and they thought timber-framed buildings from an earlier age were crude and barbaric – but they couldn't afford to replace them all. The cunning solution was to cover them with so-called 'mathematical tiles' – clay tiles shaped to look just like bricks.

A lot of new buildings were designed to be faced with these tiles right from the start. They were cheap to build and looked very smart. Royal Crescent, opposite the seafront east of the pier, is famous for them.

The tiles are usually the colour of red bricks, but some are black and others yellow (though architects call them 'white'). Brighton and Lewes have more of them than anywhere else.

Here's a tip for M-tile hunters: they have little depth, so take a close look at the 'bricks' at the corner of a building – they're quite a give-away.

Another clever wheeze

An 18th-century house off Duke Street, in the Old Town, has walls covered in wood blocks to imitate stone. Sadly, it is in a walled yard and not clearly visible from the street.

Work began in 1823. Five years later only eleven houses were occupied, and in 1837 Kemp fled the country to escape all the people he owed money. He died in Paris, perhaps having committed suicide.

• Brunswick Town
To match Kemp Town in the east, Busby now created the stunning Brunswick estate on the flat, unoccupied land just over the border in Hove.

The facilities included a market hall, but this wasn't a success and by 1840 it had become a riding school. (Today it's The Old Market theatre.)

You know you've travelled from an old town to a new one as soon as you enter Hove. Busby and his fellow architects had no inconvenient old buildings in their way and could fashion long, straight avenues as far as the eye could see. Hove, at last, was on the up.

The Pepper Pot

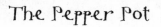

Here's a different sort of
architectural style altogether
– the Italianate.

You'll find the Pepper Pot,
as it's affectionately
called, just north of
Queen's Park. It was
part of a large villa
built for Thomas
Attree in 1830.
Its architect was
Charles Barry, who
designed the Houses
of Parliament (as
well as St Peter's
church in Brighton).

When the villa was
demolished in 1972, the Pepper
Pot survived. It was probably built as a water
tower, but it's had a wide range of other uses
since:

- An observation tower
- A scout hut
- An artist's studio
- A printworks for the *Brighton Daily Mail*.

What would you use it for?

All fall down

What a sad little story this is!

Henry Phillips, one of the leading plant experts of his day, had a brilliant idea: he'd build a vast structure of glass and iron, wider than the dome of St Peter's in Rome – indeed, the largest dome in all the world – and inside it he'd create a tropical wonderland. It would be called the Anthaeum, after the Greek word for 'flower'.

Amon Henry Wilds was brought in to design it, and in 1832 the brick foundations were laid in what are now the gardens of Palmeira Square, facing the sea.

The dome began to take shape, and among those who came to visit it was Joseph Paxton, who would later build the famous Crystal Palace in London. If he was looking for lessons, he was about to be given a very powerful one...

Wilds and his structural engineer argued that the dome needed a central column, and when the builder (a Mr English) insisted that no kind of internal bracing was needed, they immediately resigned from the project.

On 31 August 1833, the day before the official opening, the internal scaffolding was removed. Everything was ready for the grand occasion.

Sadly, Mr English's confidence proved to be without foundation.

That evening, an hour after the workmen had left, the superintendent (the only person remaining inside) heard an ominous creaking. He dashed outside — moments before the whole edifice crashed to the ground in a heap of glass and mangled iron.

Poor Henry Phillips was so shocked by the destruction of his dream that he went blind.

In a drought, they say, you can still see the outlines of the Anthaeum in the parched grass.

The Chain Pier

Piers are now a familiar part of the English seaside scene, but one of the very first was Brighton's Chain Pier,[1] which opened in 1823. It was opposite New Steine, a few blocks east of the present pier.

Once the Napoleonic Wars were over, there was a lot more to-ing and fro-ing between Brighton and France, and the main purpose of the pier was to allow passengers to get on and off steamships without having to be ferried to the beach in rowing boats. But very soon the Fashion discovered how pleasant it was to promenade along the decking, and a new entertainment was born.

Once the West Pier was built, the Chain Pier lost its popularity. It closed in October 1896, and two months later it was completely destroyed by a terrible storm.

1. The walkway hung from chains, like a suspension bridge.

After Prinny

The next king – George's brother, William IV – was rather partial to the Pavilion himself, staying there at least once every year during his reign (1830–1837). A few fascinating facts about William:

• After George's excesses he was regarded as practically teetotal – after all, he drank only a pint of sherry with his dinner.

• Prone to eccentric behaviour, he had a habit of spitting in public.

• Having served in the Royal Navy, he became known as the 'Sailor King'. And at one New Year's Eve ball he took to the dance floor partnered by a 61-year-old admiral.

• This doesn't mean what you think, because he had 12 children.

• Unfortunately, all the ones who lived to adulthood were by an actress called Dorothea Jordan, rather than William's lawful wife – so none could inherit the throne.

Queen Victoria
sells the Pavilion
and takes with
her the furniture,
fixtures and fittings
– the lot!

Enter Queen Victoria

In 1837 William IV died and his young niece Victoria came to the throne. She was just 18, and a very lively creature – nothing like the grumpy-looking old woman that we're used to seeing in photographs.

But Brighton did make her rather grumpy. She didn't like being gawped at whenever she came down to her palace by the sea.

She did give it a try. She paid her first visit within months of becoming queen, and she stayed here several more times (once landing at the Chain Pier from France) until 1845, when she decided that Osborne House on the Isle of Wight was a more pleasant place to stay.

Victoria sold the Royal Pavilion to the local council in 1850, and her lasting memories of Brighton were probably of a place too bustling for comfort.

It was about to get a lot busier!

Preston Manor

Preston Manor is just north of Brighton, on the road to London. How old is it? Well, that depends which part of it you're talking about:

- **13th century.** There are the remains of a two-roomed building in the basement.

- **16th century.** Two old doorways survive in the basement, too.

- **18th century.** Thomas Western rebuilt the house above the main floor of the medieval building, and put up small pavilions on either side of the main block.

- **20th century.** In 1905 the house was enlarged, with a dining room and servants' wing being added and a veranda gracing the north front.

So what you see today is the home of a well-to-do family in the Edwardian era.

For many visitors the fascinating parts of the house are the servants' quarters, the butler's pantry, the maids' room and the kitchen – which remain just as they were.

In the garden there's a pets' cemetery. Here you'll find the graves of a Town Hall cat, a Pavilion cat and poor Sooty, 'who was cruelly poisoned'.

Bump in the night! The White Lady, 400 years old, is only one of the many ghosts that are said to haunt Preston Manor.

Nonsense, my dear, the servants will be perfectly comfortable in Third Class.

CHAPTER four

THE RAILWAY AGE

I n 1841 the first train steamed down the line from London Bridge to Brighton,[1] and life was never the same again. Just compare the old transport with the new:

• The record time for a London–Brighton stagecoach run (in February 1834) was 3 hours 40 minutes. Most took quite a bit longer. Express trains were soon completing the journey in 1 hour 45 minutes.

• On 25 October 1833 a fleet of stagecoaches brought 480 visitors to the town – a record for

1. *Victoria station was not opened until 1858.*

one day. But on Easter Monday 1844 a single train (with four locomotives hauling at least 40 carriages) carried 1,100 passengers.

Although some people found these hissing monsters dirty and frightening, they couldn't deny that travel had become both quicker and cheaper overnight. It wasn't only the Fashion who could enjoy Brighton now, but ordinary men and women and their children – many of whom had never had a glimpse of the sea in their lives before.

Pity the poor horses

In the heyday of the stagecoaches (or 'flying machines'), different companies competed with each other to carry their passengers fastest between London and Brighton. This was bad news for the exhausted horses which had to pull them non-stop. In a single week in 1816, no fewer than 15 horses died – and after this new rules were brought in to protect them.

It was good news, too, for wealthy people who wanted to live by the coast and still keep an eye on their businesses and investments in London. Now they could pop up to the capital whenever they wished – commuting had arrived!

A great many of the substantial buildings we know in Brighton today date from the long reign of Queen Victoria (1837–1901) and the short one of Edward VII (1901–1910).

When Victoria came to the throne, Brighton and Hove spread about 4 km (2½ miles) along the coast between Kemp Town and Brunswick. By the time she died, developers had filled in nearly all the gaps and created sprawling suburbs.

You obviously can't wait for some more population figures at this point, so here we go:

	Brighton	*Hove*
1841	47,000	2,500
1861	78,000	10,000
1881	99,000	20,000
1901	123,000	36,000

Building the railway

It's easy to take it for granted today, but it was a mammoth task driving a railway line down to the coast through the sandstone of the Weald and the chalk of the Downs.

A few facts and figures:

- The line was 66 km (41 miles) long.
- 6,206 navvies and 960 horses were involved in the work.
- They had to dig five tunnels, the longest three lit by gas.
- 11 million bricks were used to build the Ouse Valley viaduct between Balcombe and Haywards Heath, with its 37 arches.
- Building Brighton Station alone required 3,500 men and 570 horses.
- The whole line was completed in just three and a half years.

White-knuckle rides

You didn't get a very comfortable ride for your money in the early days – especially if you were one of the poorer people who travelled Third Class.

You'd be crowded into an open carriage on hard seats, and you'd be horribly exposed to dust, smoke, noise and drifting specks of ash and soot. Just imagine what those tunnels must have been like!

Brighton's mini railways

The Victorians were an inventive and energetic lot, as we shall see. Among the cleverest of them was the son of a German clockmaker, Magnus Volk. We know him best for his electric railway – the very first in the world – which still runs east of the Palace Pier

The Clayton Tunnel Disaster

A signalling mix-up led to a dreadful crash in the Clayton Tunnel, 8 km (5 miles) north of Brighton, on Sunday, 25 August 1861.

No train was supposed to enter the tunnel until the one before had come out, but on this occasion three trains headed north out of Brighton within a few minutes of each other – and two of them collided inside the tunnel. Twenty-three people were killed and 176 were injured – and no help came for more than half an hour.

Magnus Volk's oddest invention

towards Black Rock. But that wasn't all. He lit his house in Dyke Road with electricity, and soon afterwards did the same for the Royal Pavilion. He also introduced the first telephone service to Brighton.

But these Victorian inventors could be pretty eccentric, too, and Volk's weirdest claim to fame was the so-called Daddy Long Legs – an electric contraption which carried passengers on stilts high above the waves as it ran to Rottingdean on underwater rails.

Murder in the Balcombe Tunnel

On the afternoon of Monday, 27 June 1881, a young man named Percy Lefroy staggered off an express train at Brighton, covered in blood.

He told station staff that he had been shot, but the truth was that Lefroy himself had just killed the 64-year-old coin dealer Frederick Gold while the train was deep in the Balcombe Tunnel. This 'railway murder' became notorious; the *Daily Telegraph* called it 'one of the most astonishingly cruel and cold-blooded assassinations of modern times'.

Because of bungling by a detective called Holmes (quite clearly not Sherlock), he managed to escape, but he was eventually captured and brought to trial.

A vain man, Lefroy asked permission to wear full evening dress in court, because he thought this would impress the jury. This request was refused, although he was allowed to carry his silk hat – and appeared to take more interest in it than he did in the court proceedings.

He was hanged at Lewes.

While we're on the subject of railways, this is the place to mention the one that ran from Hove to Devil's Dyke, with its station about 200 metres (220 yards) below the hotel. You can still make out where the buffers would have been.

Brightonians loved an excursion up to the Dyke, and there they could have even more fun by riding an aerial cableway across the gap and descending the steep northern slope of the Downs to Poynings on a funicular (cable-operated railway). What larks!

Cholera

Mind you, some of them had good reason to escape from the mean streets down below, because the poorer, horribly overcrowded parts of Brighton had become festering slums.

Thousands of people were crammed into badly constructed houses which sat alongside piggeries and slaughterhouses.

In June 1849 the civil engineer Edward Cresy arrived in the town to begin an official sanitary inspection – and that very month the first victims of Brighton's cholera outbreak fell ill and died.

The authorities were so worried that news of the disease would have a damaging effect on the tourist industry that they hushed it up. No, let's be frank: they lied about it.

The death records in the St Nicholas parish register simply have small crosses next to the names of the cholera victims – 175 of them in that first year alone – and not until 1854 is the cross replaced by a large C.

But no wonder it spread so terribly. You have only to consider the living conditions:

- **Brighton had 64 km (40 miles) of streets but only 10 km (6 miles) of sewers.**
- **During heavy rain the privies (shared outside lavatories) overflowed and contaminated the well water.**
- **In lower areas the houses often had 'material' (we can all guess what that means) saturating the foundations and oozing through the walls.**
- **800 deaths a year were caused by diseases which could have been prevented by proper sanitary measures.**

Some of the worst areas were around Albion Hill, Carlton Hill, Edward Street, Russell Street and Church Street. Dr William Kebbell, who conducted his own investigation in 1848, reported that the conditions here were 'a disgrace to any civilised people'.

Hoorah for Hawkshaw

But the Victorians could work wonders when they set their minds to it, and in 1874 Sir John Hawkshaw designed a great brick-lined sewer, 11 km (7 miles) long, to carry all the nastiness safely away to sea at Portobello, near Telscombe Cliffs. (Safely, that is, unless you swam anywhere near Portobello, because it was raw sewage that dropped into the waves – it would be another hundred years before they sorted that little problem out.)

You can see this wonderful creation for yourself during the Brighton Festival in May, when the sewers are open for guided tours. The cylindrical tunnels are large enough to stand up in – and they're not as pongy as you might think.

Visiting sewers –

– an experience not to be sniffed at

Clean water

Meanwhile they decided to do something about the water supply, which was not only contaminated but hopelessly inadequate for the ever-growing town.

The Goldstone pumping station in Hove is another fine example of the handiwork of these brilliant engineers. From 1866, a huge, steam-driven beam engine, turning with scarcely a sound, pumped water from a natural reservoir 50 metres (160 feet) deep in the chalk.

A few years later the waterworks was extended in order to supply some of the local villages. By now there were two beam engines at work, pumping all of 682,000 litres (150,000 gallons) an hour.

The pumping station is now the British Engineerium, a museum of steam engines and other industrial marvels. It closed in 2006 but is expected to re-open.

In the grounds are some creeper-covered flint arches which frame a small, scalloped cavern. An ancient grotto? No! When wells were sunk in the 1860s, the chief water engineer decided to create a 'folly' from all the flints that came up in the chalk.

Grave concerns

Another move the Victorians made to improve public health was to close graveyards in the centres of towns and cities and create new ones on the outskirts.

The private Extra-Mural Cemetery (it means 'outside the walls') was laid out in 1850, complete with underground catacombs and large family mausoleums, and it soon had a new neighbour – the parish burial ground, which we now know as Woodvale. With the Brighton & Preston Cemetery and the Lawn Memorial Park, these form an attractive, semi-wild 'valley of the dead'.

An artificial spa

The little building with columns in the corner of Queen's Park is all that's left of the grandly named Royal German Spa. Brighton didn't have natural mineral waters like those in St Ann's Well Gardens in Hove, so a Dr Struve from Dresden added various minerals to local water instead. He opened his spa in 1825, and it did good business until 1866.

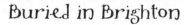

Buried in Brighton

You'll find monuments in Brighton to many of the people mentioned in this book. St Nicholas's churchyard alone has the tombs of Martha Gunn, Phoebe Hessel, Nicholas Tettersell, Amon Wilds and Sake Dean Mahomed, to mention just a few. Here are some less well-known ones to look out for:

1. **John Urpeth Rastrick.** The engineer of the London–Brighton railway line has a massive, but rather dull, tomb in the Extra-Mural Cemetery. The inscription, of course, is in Latin.

2. **Fred Ginnett.** But this one, not far away in Woodvale, is much more interesting. Ginnett was a Victorian circus proprietor, based at the 1600-seater Royal Hippodrome in Park Crescent Place, and his tomb has a bowing circus horse on top.

3. **Sir George Everest.** Buried in the churchyard of St Andrew's in Church Road, Hove, is the former surveyor-general of India – who gave his name to the highest mountain in the world.

4. **Sir George Westphal.** Buried in the same churchyard as Everest is a former young midshipman on HMS *Victory* who was wounded at the same time as Admiral Nelson during the Battle of Trafalgar. Nelson's jacket was used as a pillow for Westphal's head, and part of an epaulette (shoulder ornament) became embedded in the wound. After it was cut away, Westphal kept it for ever as a treasured memento.

5. **Anna Maria Crouch.** 'Beautiful almost beyond parallel' reads her epitaph in St Nicholas's churchyard. Born in 1763, she was one of the most famous actresses and singers of her day.

6. **Celia Holloway.** There's a grim plaque on the wall of St John's churchyard in Preston Village: 'Beneath this path are deposited portions of the remains...' Portions were all that was left of poor Celia, murdered and cut into pieces by her husband, who buried the evidence in a shallow grave at Lovers' Walk. He was hanged.

7. **Tom MS Highflyer.** Tom was only about 12 years old when he died, and all we know about him (from his memorial at Woodvale)

is that he was 'rescued from a slave dhow' somewhere overseas in 1866. Presumably it was the crew of the British MS (motor ship) *Highflyer* who saved him and gave him that name. They brought him to England, where he was baptised, but he died soon afterwards.

8. **Martin Leonard Landfried.** The Charge of the Light Brigade was a military disaster of 1854 about which Tennyson wrote a memorable poem. Some 118 men were killed and 127 wounded when the British cavalry charged hopelessly down a valley towards Russian guns. Landfried (buried in Hove Cemetery) was the young army trumpeter who sounded the charge.

9. **Henry Holden.** Buried in the Bear Road Cemetery, Holden was an Englishman who fought alongside General Custer at the famous Battle of Little Big Horn in 1876. Custer and half his cavalry were killed, while Holden's company was pinned down by 5,000 Sioux and Cheyenne warriors. He risked his life to fetch fresh ammunition and was later awarded the Congressional Medal of Honor.

10. **Daniel Skayles.** His stone in Patcham churchyard tells us that 34-year-old Skayles was 'unfortunately Shot on Thursday Evening Nov. 17 1796'. It doesn't tell us that he was shot while on a smuggling run.

The seafront gets a new look

The Victorians are renowned for their energy. While some of them were building railway lines, digging sewers and pumping water from underground, others were making money from a thousand and one different business enterprises. Walk along the seafront today and you'll see some of the wonders they created in the second half of the 19th century:

• The seafront road, 1822 and later

This was first created by George IV in 1822 (he was bestrewn with sugar plums at the opening, in keeping with tradition), but was steadily widened over the years and carried further seawards over the King's Road arches.

• The Birdcage Bandstand, 1884

Lovingly restored in 2009, the pretty little cast-iron bandstand opposite Bedford Square was designed by the borough surveyor, Philip Lockwood. He also converted the Dome from riding stables into an assembly hall, and made the buildings east of it into a library, museum and art gallery.

• The West Pier, 1866

This has *not* been lovingly restored. In fact, very little is left of it now – but it was the most beautiful pier in all England.

Designed by Eugenius Birch, the West Pier was a place for fashionable people to stroll and take the air. By 1916 it boasted a theatre and a concert hall. But in the 1970s it was abandoned and allowed to slump gradually into the sea. After two suspicious fires in 2003 and 2004, this Grade I listed building is now Brighton's best-loved ruin.

West Pier 1866

West Pier 2004

The murder of a police chief

The first chief constable of Brighton was Henry Solomon, and by 13 March 1844 he had been in the post for a little more than five years.

On that evening a 23-year-old man suspected of stealing was brought into the police station at the Town Hall. John Lawrence was unemployed and a bit of a layabout, but he hadn't been in serious trouble with the police before.

Solomon briefly questioned him and, as Lawrence appeared agitated, told him to sit down. Some minutes later Lawrence suddenly leapt to his feet, grabbed a poker from the fireplace and brought it down savagely on Solomon's head. He died from his injuries the following morning.

Lawrence, found guilty of murder, was the last person to be hanged in public at Horsham gaol.

Hanging's too good for him!

- **The Norfolk Hotel, 1865**
- **The Hotel Metropole, 1890**
- **The Grand Hotel, 1864**

The passenger lift allowed the development of the plush seaside hotel – and one of the very first (known as an 'ascending omnibus') was installed at the Grand. Water-powered, it enabled passengers and goods to be raised through the nine floors of this 150-room 'palace by the sea'.

A reporter for the *Brighton Herald* wrote that the visitor 'has only to take his seat (with half a dozen others) if he pleases, in a comfortable little room, and his commands will be obeyed with as much facility as were those of the Master of the Lamp or the Ring'.

Electric lifts had been invented by the time the Metropole arrived a quarter of a century later. The new hotel was built of red brick and terracotta, and was at first regarded as very ugly – breaking with the tradition of cream-fronted buildings along the front. It was the largest hotel in England outside London.

• The Palace Pier, 1899

Did you know that Brighton once, very briefly, had three piers? The Palace Pier was designed to replace the old Chain Pier, which was still standing (just) when its construction got under way.

Indeed, the storm which wrecked the Chain Pier also did a lot of damage to the new one, and it wasn't properly finished when it opened to the public in 1899.

It was an immediate success. Whereas the West Pier played the role of a sedate and elegant older sister, the Palace Pier was her bubbly little sibling, out to have a bit more flamboyant fun. She's still having it today.

- The decking is about 500 metres (1,650 feet) long.
- It's a Grade II* listed building, and still has many of its original features.
- Two of the kiosks, with fish-scale roofs, originally stood at the entrance of the Chain Pier. There's also a signal cannon from the old pier near the seaward end.
- The domed winter garden is now the Palace of Fun amusement arcade.

- It's the second most visited 'leisure facility' in the whole of England and attracts 4.5 million visitors every year.
- Since the collapse of the West Pier, the owners have rebranded it 'Brighton Pier' – although not everyone is very happy about that.

Oh, I do like to be beside the seaside...

The names on the buses (1)

Brighton & Hove's double-decker buses carry the names of many people with local connections. Here are some of those not mentioned elsewhere in the book.

Queen Adelaide. The wife of William IV. Queen's Park in Brighton and Adelaide Crescent in Hove are named after her.

Enid Bagnold. The author of *National Velvet* lived for more than 50 years at North End House in Rottingdean.

Aubrey Beardsley. When this brilliant artist died at the age of 25 he was already famous for his black-and-white illustrations in the Art Nouveau style. He was born in Buckingham Road and went to Brighton Grammar School.

Oliver Bulleid. He was one of the leading innovators in locomotive design and is remembered by railway enthusiasts for his work as mechanical engineer to the old Southern Railway.

Sir Edward Burne-Jones. A leading Victorian artist, he lived in Rottingdean and designed several fine stained-glass windows in the village church and other Brighton churches.

Sir John Cordy Burrows. Nicknamed King Cordy, he came to Brighton in 1837 and was hugely influential in the town, being made mayor three times. When he died 30,000 people lined the route of his funeral.

Ellen Nye Chart. Taking over the Theatre Royal after her husband's death in 1875, she launched a period of remarkable brilliance, attracting actors such as Sir Henry Irving and Dame Ellen Terry. Her ghost is said to haunt the theatre.

Sir Winston Churchill. The great war leader attended a school in Brunswick Road, Hove, where a fellow pupil stabbed him (not too seriously) with a penknife.

C. B. Cochran. Born in Prestonville Road in 1872, he was a great 20th-century showman, working with celebrities such as Charlie Chaplin, Will Rogers and Noël Coward.

Captain Frederick Collins. He operated his *Skylark* pleasure boats from Brighton beach, and his cry 'Any more for the *Skylark*?' became a national catch-phrase.

Syd Dean. Resident bandleader at the Regent ballroom in Queen's Road in the 1940s and 50s; his music brought many local couples together.

Stanley Deason. This former mayor was passionately committed to the cause of education, and the leisure centre in Wilson Avenue is named after him.

Charles Dickens. The author came to Brighton frequently to give readings from his books.

• The Aquarium, 1872

It's now the Sea Life Centre, and it was altered a good deal in the 1920s, but you only have to descend the steps into the main hall to admire the Victorians' eye for drama.

Its architect was Eugenius Birch, who also designed the West Pier, and he created a magical atmosphere in the dimly lit interior with its columns of red Edinburgh granite and green serpentine marble. Its central hall housed a huge tank – the largest in the world at that time – which held 500,000 litres (110,000 gallons) of water.

'Merciful Heavens,' thought Ada, 'that fish looks just like Queen Victoria.'

The early attractions included a large octopus, some sea lions and a Norway lobster. Organ recitals were put on twice a day, and there were concerts in the conservatory.

The Aquarium has had its ups and downs over the years, and the remodelling in the 1920s removed its Italianate clock tower, but today it's as popular as ever.

• Madeira Drive, 1872

The Aquarium was built over the former carriage road along the front, which meant that a new one had to be constructed to replace it.

This was Madeira Drive. Sheltered by the huge sea wall that had been raised between the Old Steine and Kemp Town during the 1830s, it became – and remains – a favourite place for promenading.

It also became a short course for motor speed trials (still held every September) and a finishing point for a variety of London-to-Brighton events.

London to Brighton

It's about 80 km (50 miles) from the capital down to Madeira Drive – an excellent length for all kinds of sporting and allied activities.

- In 1803 John Bell – the first recorded person to complete the distance – walked from London to Brighton in 13 hours 45 seconds.

- In 1872 the winner of an Amateur Bicycle Club race completed the course in 5 hours 25 minutes. Today, the British Heart Foundation's London-to-Brighton Bike Ride is a fixture in the calendar every June, with 30,000 entrants – and the leaders go rather faster than that.

- In 1877 J. Granby set out to walk to Brighton with a 50 lb (23 kg) bag of sand on his back. Unfortunately he only got as far as Thornton Heath in Surrey.

- In 1896 the Light Locomotives Act allowed vehicles to drive at a speed of 14 mph (22.5 kph), and the Motor Car Club organised a 'great procession from Whitehall to Brighton' to celebrate this heady new freedom. The Veteran Car Run is still held every November. Only vehicles made before 1905 may take part.

- The first amateur running event was a go-as-you-please contest organised by South London Harriers in 1899. The winner, F. D. Randall of Finchley Harriers, ran the distance in

6 hours 58 minutes 18 seconds. On the strength of this run, the first three men home were selected to compete for Great Britain in the 1900 Olympic marathon.

- In 1903 an American music-hall artiste, 'Miss Florence', walked to Brighton on a ball. It took her five days – but for some reason this hasn't caught on.

- One of the most colourful events is the Commercial Vehicles Road Run each May, attracting some 200 historical vans, lorries and other vehicles.

- There are separate events for Minis, Land Rovers and various other types of vehicle.

Brighton can be chilly in November.

• Madeira Terrace, 1890

Very soon afterwards the impressive Madeira Terrace was completed – stretching all of 864.7 metres (2,837 feet) from the Aquarium to Duke's Mound in the east. It's supported by cast-iron columns and has delicate latticed arches. The figures you see are, alternately, Neptune or Poseidon (god of the sea) and Venus or Aphrodite (goddess of love).

Elderly legs didn't much like the long climb from the seafront to the top road (Marine Parade), so the ornate Madeira Lift – orginally hydraulically powered – was installed at the same time.

A drop too much

You didn't have to go far for a drink if you got thirsty in Victorian times. In 1889 there were reportedly 774 beer-houses of different kinds in the town – one for every 130 residents. Many of them were to be found in the new working-class areas, such as the one between Brighton Station and London Road, where drunkenness became a serious problem.

A lot of learning

Along with public health and sanitation, education was one of the Victorians' 'big ideas'. New schools sprang up everywhere, including some which are highly regarded today.

• Brighton College dates from 1848, its first buildings designed by George Gilbert Scott.

• Brighton & Hove High School (1876), designed by Amon Wilds, occupies the former home of Thomas Read Kemp, the Temple, in Montpelier Road.

• Brighton, Hove and Sussex Sixth-Form College (BHASVIC) started life as Brighton Grammar School in the 1870s.

• Roedean, now in its famous Gothic pile on the clifftops, was founded as a small school in Kemp Town by the three Lawrence sisters in 1885.

Wagner and Wagner

But for many Victorians the biggest idea of all was religion. Brighton and Hove had their old parish churches, but many more were now needed to serve the rapidly growing population.

Two notable churchmen of the Victorian era were the Reverend Henry Wagner (vicar of Brighton from 1824 until 1870) and his son the Reverend Arthur Wagner, perpetual curate[1] to St Paul's church in West Street from 1850.

They were wealthy people who worked hard to make life better for the underprivileged. Henry Wagner himself had six churches built (including St Paul's and St John the Evangelist) because he knew that there were only 3,000 free pews in all the town's churches for 20,000 poor people.

Arthur not only paid for five churches in the poorer parts of town – the magnificent St

1. *The priest in charge of a newly created parish.*

Bartholomew's was one of them – but had 400 houses built in the Islingword Road district and the Round Hill Estate between the Lewes and Upper Lewes Roads.

But Arthur Wagner wasn't universally popular. He was an advocate of the Tractarian movement, practising what was known as Anglo-Catholicism, or (as his enemies put it) 'smells and bells religion'. He used incense, rang a small bell during communion services and heard his parishioners' confessions just as if they were in a Roman Catholic church. This brought him enemies – once he was even shot at.

A terrible confession

In 1865 a young woman entered Arthur Wagner's confessional and told him that she had killed her four-year-old half-brother with a razor. She was Constance Kent, and the murder was one of the sensations of the age. Wagner helped her give herself up to justice but caused a stir by saying he would tell the court nothing more, as he had heard her story under the seal of 'sacramental confession'. Kent was sentenced to death but was spared because of her age.

Ten places of worship

1. **St Nicholas**, Dyke Road. Brighton's ancient parish church, largely rebuilt in the 1850s, but with a 14th-century tower. Many of the town's 'great and good' are buried in the churchyard.

2. **St Bartholomew**, Ann Street. A huge, barn-like church with gorgeous richness inside. Designed for Arthur Wagner by Edmund Scott.

3. **St Michael & All Angels**, Victoria Road (off Montpelier Road). Designed by two Victorian masters, Bodley and Burges, it has stained-glass windows by Burne-Jones, Webb and Morris.

4. **All Saints**, Eaton Road, Hove. This cathedral-like building has been Hove's parish church since being built (in 13th-century style) in 1892.

5. **St Andrew**, Waterloo Street, Hove. Another Victorian masterpiece, designed in Italianate style by Charles Barry in 1828. (Not to be confused with St Andrew in Church Road, Hove's original medieval church, which was rebuilt in the 1830s.)

6. **St Paul**, West Street. Built for Arthur Wagner in 1848 as a mission church for Brighton's fishermen, it became a principal church of the Tractarian movement.

7. **Chapel Royal**, North Street. Built in a classical style in the 1790s but remodelled in Victorian times. It has the feel of a Nonconformist chapel inside.

8. **St George**, St George's Road, Kemp Town. A typical brick Regency church, with galleries inside. It has a square bell turret with a cupola (small dome).

9. **St John the Baptist**, Bristol Road, Kemp Town. The Roman Catholic church in which you'll find the monument to Mrs Fitzherbert.

10. **Middle Street Synagogue.** Dating from 1875, this is a listed building because of its sumptuous interior, with galleries supported by columns of red marble. It was the first synagogue to be lit by electricity.

St Nicholas

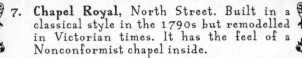

Brighton goes to the pictures

We take moving images for granted these days, but we owe today's films and TV programmes in part to several pioneers who worked in Brighton, Hove and nearby Shoreham Beach. Why here? Chiefly because the light was so good along the coast.

In 1889 William Friese-Greene patented his 'chronophotographic' camera, which could take ten photographs per second using celluloid film. On a Sunday morning in 1889 he took his new camera to Hyde Park in London and filmed pedestrians, open-topped buses and hansom cabs.

That evening he projected his film onto a small screen – and so became the very first person to witness moving pictures!

In 1894 George Albert Smith, another of the early producers, took a lease on St Ann's Well Gardens in Hove. Apart from making his films there, he introduced attractions such as a fortune teller and a hermit living in a cave.

Two years later, the first film show in Brighton (and the first in England outside London) was given at the Pandora Gallery, opposite the West Pier, using a 'cinematographe'.

In no time at all, it seemed, Brighton and Hove were at the cutting edge of the new art form. The Duke of York's Picture House at Preston Circus opened in 1910 and is now the oldest continuously operating cinema in Britain.

On the roof of the Duke of York's is a sculpture of a gigantic pair of high-kicking legs in striped stockings. This originally adorned an independent cinema in Oxford called the Moulin Rouge, which later changed its name for legal reasons to 'Not the Moulin Rouge'.

fit for an Empress

The Victorians enjoyed a show, and in 1886 an impressive Colonial and Indian Exhibition was staged at the Guildhall in London. (Queen Victoria had become Empress of India ten years earlier.)

Among the exhibits was the ornate Jaipur Gate, designed by two Englishmen but carved and assembled by Indian craftsmen – and since 1926 it has stood in the grounds of Hove Museum in New Church Road.

Made of long-lasting teak, it's decorated with finely beaten gold and bears the motto of the Maharajas of Jaipur in English, Sanskrit and Latin: 'Where virtue is, there is victory.' It was restored in 2009.

Calling time on the time ball

Trust the Victorians to make a big thing of it! The brief was to create a clock tower to commemorate Queen Victoria's golden jubilee in 1887, but once Magnus Volk was involved it became something much more elaborate than most Brightonians can have imagined.

The edifice was a gift to the town from the local advertising contractor John Willing. It has four seated female statuettes on its red granite base, while above are four mosaic portraits, including one of the Queen. Throw in columns, pediments, four projecting signposts, four clock faces and a cupola, and this is already a pretty busy composition – but there's more to come...

The time ball

Squeak

That gilt-copper sphere near the top was a 'time ball', designed by Volk to be controlled by a land-line from Greenwich Observatory and to rise up the mast on the hour. But it was very noisy, and people soon put a stop to it.

Ten films set in Brighton

1. **Bank Holiday** (1938)
2. **Brighton Rock** (1947)
3. **Genevieve** (1953)
4. **The Trials of Oscar Wilde** (1960)
5. **Jigsaw** (1962)
6. **Oh! What a Lovely War** (1969)
7. **Carry On at Your Convenience** (1971)
8. **Quadrophenia** (1979)
9. **The Ploughman's Lunch** (1983)
10. **The End of the Affair** (2000)

CHAPTER FIVE

TWO WARS AND A BIT OF PEACE

lthough the shelling, gassing and mass slaughter happened on the other side of the Channel, the horrors of the First World War were very soon brought home to the people of Brighton and Hove. It certainly *wasn't* a lovely war . . .

In 1914 the grammar school in Dyke Road (now the sixth-form college) was turned into a military hospital, and 300 wounded soldiers of the 2nd Royal Sussex Regiment were taken there. More emergency beds had to be found as the number of injured men continued to rise, and several schools and the workhouse in

Elm Grove (later Brighton General Hospital) were taken over by the military.

The Royal Pavilion, the Dome and the Corn Exchange were turned into hospitals for Indian soldiers. Perhaps they felt at home amongst Prinny's oriental creations.

The bodies of Hindu and Sikh soldiers who died while in Brighton were cremated on a *ghat* (cremation platform) high on the Downs above Patcham. After the war was over, an attractive little domed building known as the Chattri was erected there as a monument to 'all the Indian soldiers who gave their lives in the service of their King-Emperor'. A half-hour memorial service is held here in June each year – the only one of its kind in Britain. The domed South Gate of the Pavilion is another tribute. This 'gift of India in commemoration of her sons' was dedicated by the Maharaja of Patiala in 1921.

Because the carnage of the First World War had been so terrible, people called it 'the war to end wars' – but in little more than twenty years the guns would be firing all over again.

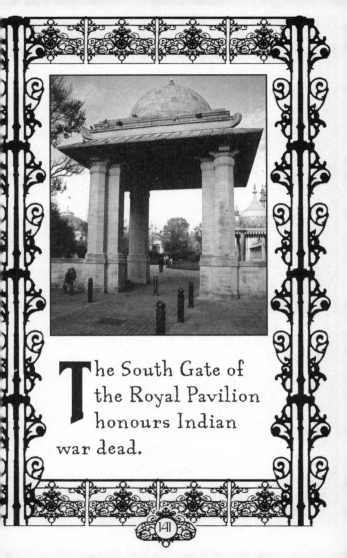

The South Gate of the Royal Pavilion honours Indian war dead.

Seedy Brighton

There was a good deal of poverty in Brighton during the 1920s and 1930s, and the town began to get a reputation for being down-at-heel and even rather dangerous.

Up at the racecourse there were brutal gangs organising betting scams and other illegal schemes, and spectators would recoil in horror when they fought each other with open razors.

It didn't help when Graham Greene's famous novel *Brighton Rock* was published in 1938. Greene later said of it, 'I must plead guilty to manufacturing this Brighton of mine as I never manufactured Mexico or IndoChina.'

Many of the locals weren't happy with his tale of Brighton's sordid underworld characters, but there's no doubt that it touched a nerve. Brighton was pretty seedy.

• The trunk murders

Nothing was nastier than two grim discoveries made within the space of a few weeks in 1934. (Do jump this page if you're squeamish.)

On 17 June an evil-smelling plywood trunk was opened at the left-luggage office of Brighton railway station. Inside was the torso of a young woman. (The legs were found in a suitcase at King's Cross station in London.)

This case was never solved, but on 15 July, while the police were still investigating it, another woman's body was found in a trunk at a house in Kemp Street.

She was Violet Kaye, and this time the police did have a suspect – her partner, Toni Mancini. In later life he admitted that he was indeed the murderer, but he was brilliantly defended in court by the lawyer Norman Birkett, and the jury incredibly found him not guilty.

Brighton had once been known as 'the queen of watering places', so what do you think the wags called her now? That's right: 'the queen of slaughtering places'. Oh dear . . .

Ten novels set* in Brighton

1. **Pride and Prejudice**
   (Jane Austen, 1813)

2. **Dombey and Son**
   (Charles Dickens, 1848)

3. **The Newcomes**
   (William Makepeace Thackeray, 1855)

4. **Ovingdean Grange**
   (William Harrison Ainsworth, 1860)

5. **New Grub Street**
   (George Gissing, 1891)

6. **Hilda Lessways**
   (Arnold Bennett, 1911)

7. **Brighton Rock**
   (Graham Greene, 1938)

8. **Hangover Square**
   (Patrick Hamilton, 1941)

9. **Sugar Rush**
   (Julie Burchill, 2004)

10. **Dead Simple**
    (Peter James, 2005)

*at least in part

The Peacehaven story

Just before the First World War, the developer Charles Neville bought up a large swathe of cliff-top downland between Brighton and Newhaven, and when the war was over he began to create his 'Lureland by the Sea' – we know it today as Peacehaven.

Neville advertised plots in the national press, and gave away many as competition prizes. People came down to the Sussex coast thinking they were going to live in paradise, but actually found mud roads and a forlorn scattering of shacks.

Horses were tethered to hitching-rails, just like the American Wild West. In those early years there was no proper drainage and residents had an electricity supply for only a few hours a day.

In Graham Green's *Brighton Rock* it's portrayed as a fitting place for a murder: 'It was like the last effort of despairing pioneers to break new country. The country had broken them.'

Peacehaven long had the reputation of being a planner's worst nightmare – but it's a cheery enough place today.

The names on the buses (2)

Tommy Farr. British heavyweight champion who narrowly lost a fight to the famous Joe Louis in 1937. When he retired from the ring he ran the Royal Standard pub in Queen's Road.

Edwin Fownes. Born in 1851 and based in Brighton, Fownes was the most famous four-in-hand coachman in the days of the London–Brighton stagecoaches. He lived until 1943, when cars were king.

C. B. Fry. Probably the greatest sporting all-rounder ever. He held the world long-jump record, appeared in an FA cup final, played rugby for the Barbarians, captained Oxford University at cricket, football and athletics in the same year, and captained both Sussex and England at cricket. He wrote several books and stood as a Liberal candidate at elections in Brighton. Oh, and he also once turned down the throne of Albania – or so he claimed.

Baron Goldsmid. Isaac Lyon Goldsmid was the first Jew to be created a baronet. In 1830 he bought the Wick estate in Hove and developed the Grade I buildings of Adelaide Crescent and Palmeira Square.

Gilbert Harding. Once called 'the rudest man in Britain', he hosted the radio quiz show *Twenty Questions*. He lived in the Montpelier district of Brighton for many years.

Sir Rowland Hill. The man who invented the penny post, while Secretary to the Post Office in the 1850s, lived at Hanover Crescent. He was also a director of the London, Brighton & South Coast Railway.

Albert Ketèlbey. The first millionaire composer, he became leader of the West Pier orchestra in the 1920s.

Rudyard Kipling. The famous author lived at Rottingdean – until gawping tourists drove him away to Burwash.

David Land. The impresario made a fortune by discovering the songwriting team of Tim Rice and Andrew Lloyd Webber, who wrote *Jesus Christ Superstar* and *Evita*. He ran Brighton's Theatre Royal for more than ten years.

Harry Leader. The son of a Russian Army trumpeter, he was resident bandleader at the Regent Ballroom between 1953 and 1963. He wrote more than 350 songs, many with his wife Rona (the best-known is 'Little Man, You've Had a Busy Day'), and sold millions of records.

Bobby Lee. He became a superstar playing ice hockey for the Brighton Tigers both before and after the Second World War.

Ida Lupino. A member of a famous theatrical family known as the 'royal family of greasepaint', she was brought up in Hove. She acted, directed and produced films and television series.

Carden saves the day

At this low point in the town's fortunes a visionary character came to the rescue. Herbert Carden (1867–1941) believed in what he called 'municipal socialism' – the idea that Brighton council should involve itself in a wide range of activities to improve day-to-day life for the people. He did so much during his time as a councillor and alderman that he was later dubbed 'the maker of modern Brighton'.

Carden's influence was felt even before the First World War, although his vigour and inspiration were vital in the years that followed it. Here are a few of the things he helped to drive along:

• **Trams**
Brighton's electric tramway system was launched in 1901, and within a few years there were 50 cars – several illuminated by coloured bulbs – travelling on just under 16 km (10 miles) of track. From the Steine it was an eight-minute journey to the station and 18 minutes up to Race Hill. Buses eventually took over, and the trams disappeared in 1939.

From the Steine to the station in style – in 8 minutes!

Killed by a tram

Brighton's trams had an excellent safety record overall, but at 7 o'clock on a blustery December morning in 1935 the brakes failed on a no. 74 as it ran along the steep part of Ditchling Road north of the Level. It jumped the points at Union Road and overturned. Twenty-four people were injured, and a cyclist hit by the tram was killed.

Phone boxes

There aren't many of the old-style red telephone boxes left from the 1930s, but look out for them in Dyke Road (near St Nicholas church), New Road, Pelham Square, Powis Square, St Peter's Place and Upper North Street.

• **Telephones**

Magnus Volk (of course) had the first phone, connecting his house in Preston Road to that of a friend nearby, but the first municipal telephone system was installed in 1903, with an exchange by the Palace Pier. By the following year there were 750 subscribers.

• Water supply

The pumping staton in Lewes Road had to be closed in 1903 because its source had become contaminated. This problem would obviously get worse if land was developed near water supplies, so Carden bought up large areas of downland and sold it to Brighton Corporation at the price he paid for it.

• Greater Brighton

On 1 April 1928 Brighton expanded five-fold, taking in Ovingdean, Rottingdean, most of Falmer and parts of Patcham and West Blatchington.

There were week-long celebrations, including a visit by the Duke and Duchess of York (later George VI and Queen Elizabeth), who unveiled the pylons at the entrance to the enlarged borough on the A23. On one of the pylons you'll find (if you're daft enough to brave the traffic) this welcome to all who drive into the town:

Hail guest, we ask not what thou art.
If friend we greet thee hand and heart.
If stranger such no longer be.
If foe our love shall conquer thee.

• **New buildings for old**

Herbert Carden, knighted in 1930 for his many services to Brighton, helped spur the redevelopment of run-down parts of the town – and he loved the 'modernist' style most of all. Embassy Court, on the seafront opposite the Peace Statue, is a typical 1930s building, looking something like a great ocean liner. Sir Herbert defended it against its many critics, but we can be pleased that there were a few things on his wish-list that he *failed* to bring about:

• **To rebuild the whole seafront from Kemp Town to Hove in Embassy Court style.**
• **To redevelop the Lanes.**
• **To knock down the Royal Pavilion and replace it with a conference and entertainment centre.**

A *lively* hotelier

This is a good point to introduce Harry Preston (1860–1936), a contemporary of Carden who also had a great influence on the town – although in a very different way. He came to Brighton in 1901 when it was a resort in decline, the Fashion having been replaced by day-trippers. Sir Harry, as he became, was to bring in the fashionable types of the new age.

Preston first bought the near-derelict Royal York Hotel (now Royal York Buildings) on the south side of the Steine, and then the Royal Albion Hotel next door. Having refurbished his hotels, and made a great splash about them in the national newspapers, he brought the leading film stars, authors and sportsmen of the day down to Brighton – making it fashionable all over again.

A keen sportsman, he loved boxing (he'd done a bit of it himself at bantamweight), motor racing and flying, and he persuaded the council to tarmac Madeira Drive so that it could be used for motor racing. A 'Motor Race Week' was held in July 1905, when the highest speed recorded was 90.2 miles an hour (145 kph) – only 15 mph (24 kph) slower than the world land speed record at the time.

Sir Harry put on charity shows at the Dome, where boxers such as Jack Dempsey and Bombardier Billy Wells performed, and for a time Brighton was bright and bustling again.

Another war

But once more the clouds of war had begun to gather. The First World War, however terrible its effects, was a distant affair for the people of Brighton and Hove, but the second one exploded all around them.

A night-time blackout was enforced in August 1939, and air-raid shelters were dug in school playgrounds and parks. In 1940 the beaches were closed to the public, and children were evacuated to other, safer parts of the country. Both the piers were partly dismantled so they could not be used for enemy landings.

The first air raid came on 15 July 1940, and they were to be a continual threat until the very last one on 22 March 1944.

In Brighton's heaviest air raid, on 25 May 1943, the town was dive-bombed by enemy fighters, which strafed pedestrians in the street. Twenty-four people were killed and 51 seriously injured.

Brighton beach in 1940: getting into the sea is still an assault course today.

During the Second World War, Brighton alone (not counting Hove) suffered:

- 56 air raids
- 1,058 siren warnings
- 685 local alarms
- 381 high-explosive bombs
- 198 people killed
- 357 people seriously injured
- 433 people slightly injured
- 200 houses destroyed
- 894 houses seriously damaged
- 14,232 houses slightly damaged
- serious damage to the London Road railway viaduct and part of the railway works
- a direct hit on the Black Rock gasworks.

The Odeon Cinema attack

On the afternoon of Saturday 14 September 1940, the Odeon Cinema in St George's Road, Kemp Town, was packed with families watching a film called *The Ghost Comes Home* when a German Dornier aircraft dropped a bomb on it. There was panic in the darkness. Two adults, a teenager and a six-year-old girl were killed outright. Many others were wounded, and six more children and four adults later died of their injuries in hospital.

Celebrations – and after

You can imagine the joy on Victory in Europe Day, 8 May 1945. The mayor read a victory proclamation from the Town Hall balcony, bonfires were lit on the Downs and on the beaches, and street parties were arranged all over the town.

And yet Brighton, perhaps inevitably, took a long time to recover its spirit after the war was over. Its energies were spent, and people had very little money.

There was a limited range of food available, and not very much of what you *could* buy. Families were rationed to a certain amount every week; meat was limited in this way until as late as July 1955.

It was only in the 1960s that prosperity began to return, and – for this book at least – this is when we arrive in modern Brighton.

The names on the buses (3)

Trevor Mann. A children's doctor who saved the lives of many babies, he founded the baby-care unit which bears his name at the Royal Sussex County Hospital.

Gideon Mantell. He discovered the bones of the dinosaur he called *Iguanodon* in Sussex. Moving from Lewes to the Old Steine in 1833, he opened his collection of fossils to the public.

Sir Edward Marshall-Hall. Born in Brighton, he became one of the most famous barristers of his day and was known as The Great Defender.

Max Miller. There's a statue in New Road to the Cheeky Chappie, as this star of the music hall was known. He died in 1963.

David Mocatta. Architect to the London, Brighton & South Coast Railway, he designed Brighton railway station and rebuilt the old synagogue in Devonshire Place.

Dr Clifford Musgrave. He was director of the Royal Pavilion after the Second World War and persuaded the council to restore it. A founder member of the Regency Society, he wrote a book entitled *Life in Brighton*.

Dame Anna Neagle. Married to film director Herbert Wilcox, the famous actress lived in Lewes Crescent. She made her last film in 1959.

Ray Noble. The great British bandleader was born in Brighton in 1903, and he became the first to succeed in America.

Sir Arthur Pearson. He founded St Dunstan's centre for the war-blinded, first in London and later in Brighton. His widow laid the foundation stone of the current building at Ovingdean.

Margaret Powell. The author of *Below Stairs* lived in Old Shoreham Road, Hove, and was 'discovered' late in life by the BBC.

Douglas Reeve. Born in the Lanes, and known in his youth as The Wonder Boy Organist, he was a regular on BBC radio's *Tuesday Night at the Dome*, which ran for 1600 performances.

Dame Flora Robson. One of the famous stage and screen actors attracted to Brighton after the Second World War, she made the town her permanent home.

Dorothy Stringer. A councillor, alderman and mayor of Brighton, she served for all of 50 years on the education committee without missing a meeting. A school is named after her.

Sir Charles Thomas-Stanford. The owner of Preston Manor, he left it to Brighton Corporation on his death in 1932.

Allen West. His electrical engineering firm was the biggest company in Brighton in the 1960s – and is still thriving today.

How to make a stick of Brighton rock

Here's how seaside rock is made. It requires high temperatures and specialised equipment, so

DON'T TRY THIS AT HOME!

- Boil water, sugar and glucose syrup in a copper pan to about 146°C (295°F).
- Tip the contents onto a lipped boiling table.
- Take some of the toffee-like gloop to a machine that will mix it with air and add flavouring.
- Mix the rest of it with the colour of your choice – traditionally red. This will form the letters and the outer casing.
- Now for the clever bit. Form strips of the red and white mixtures and layer them together to create the red letters and the white spaces between them. Make your stick of rock *much bigger* than the ones they sell in the shops, so the letters are at least 25 mm (one inch) high.
- Put the core of the rock and the lettering together. This makes a huge lump which looks more like a suet pudding than a stick of rock.
- Finally, pull the rock into long strings and snip it with a scissor-like tool. The pulling stretches out the rock until it is no more than 25 mm thick, and the letters are about 3 mm high. Everyone will wonder how you made the letters so neat and tiny.

MODERN BRIGHTON

A common joke about the 1960s is that 'If you remember them you weren't there.' The idea is that people who really got the most out of that exciting decade were too befuddled to have the slightest memory of it.

It's nonsense, of course – but there's no doubt that Brighton gradually grew more prosperous after the drab postwar years.

Teenagers in particular felt a new sense of freedom, partly because they had more money in their pockets and partly because this bright new world of coffee bars and rock music seemed to have been created especially for them. After all, they now had the Beatles, rather than the fuddy-duddy dance bands their parents listened to.

Mind you, some good things were lost:

• The Regent Cinema
This was on the corner of Queen's Road and North Street, where Boots is today. The upstairs ballroom was where hundreds of Brighton couples first met and danced the night away. The ballroom was turned into a bingo hall in 1967, and the cinema itself closed six years later.

• SS Brighton
This popular sports stadium in West Street staged wrestling, judo, basketball and professional tennis, and was home to the Brighton Tigers ice-hockey team. It was closed down in 1965 by the company which developed the Kingswest centre next door.

• Trolleybuses
These handsome creatures ran on rubber tyres like ordinary buses, but were powered by electricity from overhead cables. The trouble

was that the two poles that drew the supply down to the motor kept coming off the wires. The buses were, in short, rather cumbersome – and the last one ran in June 1961.

• The Bedford Hotel

The original Bedford Hotel, built in 1835, was regarded as the finest late-Georgian building in Brighton after the Royal Pavilion. Charles Dickens wrote *Dombey and Son* while staying there.

Destroyed by fire in 1964, it was replaced by the present 17-storey block – which is just what some councillors had wanted all along. 'What the dickens do we want to preserve an out-of-date hotel for?' one of them asked.

• The *Brighton Belle*

This luxury Pullman train used to run three times a day between London and the coast. In 1970 British Rail decided to take kippers off the breakfast menu, and there was a huge protest by celebrities such as the actor Lord Olivier. The protesters won that battle, but two years later BR decided that the *Brighton Belle* was too expensive to run, and they withdrew it.

Churchill Square

Typical of this brave new world was the new Churchill Square shopping precinct, which opened in 1968. A lot of buildings had to be demolished to make way for it, including an early 19th-century street of cobble-fronted buildings, Grenville Place.

They liked obliterating the past during the 1960s. In 1961 Brighton Council decided to issue a compulsory purchase order so that they could knock down the Grand Hotel and turn it into an amusement centre. Thank goodness the Government slapped a listed building notice on it just in time!

The precinct was very ugly. They liked putting up what were known as 'brutal' buildings in the 1960s – usually of concrete, and the taller the better. Sussex Heights, behind the Hotel Metropole, is regarded by many as the very worst of them. It has 24 floors, rises to 112 metres (336 feet) and sticks out along the seafront like a sore and squared-off thumb.

Churchill Square also sported a large, ugly, jagged piece of sculpture (concrete, of course) called for some reason *The Spirit of Brighton*.

The whole complex was pulled down and refashioned in the late 1990s.

The universities

The first 52 students enrolled at the University of Sussex's Falmer campus in October 1961. It was the very first of a new crop of 'red-brick' universities throughout Britain.

Sir Basil Spence designed the first buildings, but growth has continued ever since and the university now has more than 12,000 students.

Sussex University's (optimistic) motto is 'Be still and know'.

The former polytechnic became the University of Brighton in 1992.

Mods and Rockers

On May Bank Holiday 1964, running battles on Brighton seafront confirmed all the awful things that older people believed about 'youth today'. These skirmishes were between Mods (who wore smart clothes and rode about on motor scooters) and Rockers (who looked tough, wore leathers and rode motorbikes).

Hundreds of deckchairs were broken and beach pebbles were thrown as thousands of spectators looked on. About 150 police officers (and one horse) eventually got things under control, and 26 young people were later given stiff sentences in the courts.

Built to last?

The architectural writer Sir Nikolaus Pevsner described Hove's Victorian Town Hall as 'so red, so Gothic, so hard, so imperishable'. Unfortunately, on 9 January 1966 – only a few weeks after he had written those words – the building went up in flames. Firemen rescued six people trapped inside, but the Town Hall was in ruins. Alas, its modern replacement isn't as universally loved.

Brighton's Bank Holiday riots inspired the cult film *Quadrophenia*, released in 1979.

The conference trade

Britain was growing more prosperous with each decade. This meant that many people who usually took their holidays at the seaside could now – for the first time – afford to fly off to sunny places overseas that many of them had never even heard of before. For Brighton this posed a problem: how could it attract more visitors?

The answer was to bring in politicians and business people who needed a pleasant place to run their annual conferences. After all, most of them had their husbands or wives in tow, and they'd fancy a walk along the promenade or a visit to the shops while their partners were doing the boring things.

The Brighton Centre, which opened on the seafront in September 1977, was designed to cater not only for conferences, but for sporting events and concerts, too. In October it welcomed Bing Crosby, who gave what was to be the last performance of his life. Many other famous bands and artists have followed him over the years.

168

The Grand Hotel bomb

The Conservative Party was gathered for its annual conference in Brighton in October 1984 when the IRA (which sought to drive the British out of Northern Ireland) detonated a bomb in the Grand Hotel.

When it went off just before 3.00am, the hard-working prime minister, Margaret Thatcher, was still up, preparing for the following day's business. She survived – and addressed the conference that day as planned – but five people were killed and another 34 were injured.

The hotel was later renovated and extended – and Mrs Thatcher herself officially reopened it in August 1986.

Brighton Marina

The first proposal for what we would now call a marina in Brighton was put forward at least 200 years ago, but it took the pugnacity of a garage proprietor called Henry Cohen to finally get one built.

His first plans were for a 'city by the sea' which would include – take a deep breath –

3,000 yacht berths, helicopter and hovercraft stations, flats, a hotel, restaurants, shops, clubs, a conference hall, a swimming pool, a bowling alley, a theatre, cinemas, a casino and car parks.

He wanted to build it to the west of Duke's Mound, which offended the good citizens of Kemp Town, so the location was switched further east, to Black Rock.

Here, on 31 May 1979, the new marina was officially opened by Queen Elizabeth II – although, after years of squabbles, enquiries and compromises, it wasn't quite as Henry Cohen had imagined it.

The concrete entrance to the marina is hideous, and other parts of it are grim, but there are plans (when money allows) for a major revamp.

Covering a total of 51 hectares (126 acres), the marina complex contains 1,600 berths and 863 houses. It also has the largest non-industrial lock in Europe, measuring 100 by 10 metres (328 by 33 feet).

Brighton gets the credit

Brighton isn't noted as a commercial centre, so the decision of the giant credit-card firm American Express to built its European headquarters in Edward Street came as a great boost back in 1977.

Nine-storey Amex House, with its blue-tinted glass windows, is affectionately known as 'the wedding cake'. Some 2,000 people work in it.

This sporting life

Brighton and Hove have had their fair share of sporting heroes in recent years:

• **Cricket**
The county cricket team was founded in 1839, but had to wait until 2003 to win the championship for the very first time – and then won it in 2006 and 2007, too.

• **Athletics**
The Brighton middle-distance runner Steve Ovett was a world record holder and Olympic

gold medallist in the 1970s and early 1980s. He was honoured by a statue in Preston Park, but thieves stole it (probably in order to melt it down), leaving only his feet behind.

• Boxing
Chris Eubank, a local character with a flamboyant taste in clothes and a love of outsize cars, won 45 of his 52 professional fights, holding first the world middleweight title and then the super-middleweight title.

• Football
Brighton and Hove Albion, alias 'the Seagulls', played in the top division of the Football League (now the Premiership) from 1979 until they were relegated in 1983 – the year in which they reached the Cup Final against Manchester United, narrowly missed a last-minute winner and then lost 4–0 in the replay.

In the 1990s fans were disgusted to learn that the club's directors had sold the Goldstone Ground in Hove to developers, and there were emotional scenes when Stuart Storer scored the very last goal there at the end of the 1996–1997 season. The Seagulls played in Gillingham,

Kent, for two seasons before coming back to Brighton and using the old sports arena at Withdean. A brand-new stadium at Falmer opened in July 2011.

Alternative Brighton

Brighton has always had much to offer to those outside the mainstream.

• Gay Brighton

Kemp Town in particular has long been a magnet for the gay community – which in Brighton, at least, is no longer regarded as being on the fringe at all – and there are pubs, clubs and 'pink parlours' galore.

• Entertainments

The Komedia in Gardner Street offers European café-style live entertainment, with a mixture of comedy, music and cabaret, together with a streetside café.

• Shops

Specialist outlets in the North Laine area cater for everything from 'cruelty-free' footwear to juggling equipment.

Celebrations

Brighton continues to attract actors, artists, journalists and other creative types. This is because it's never lost its flair, or its appetite for having a good time at the smallest excuse. Here are just three annual events which get the crowds out:

• Brighton Festival

Every May the town is crammed with people attending plays, concerts, readings, exhibitions and street events. It's the biggest arts festival in England – and it's still growing.

• Burning the Clocks

Brighton has its own fire festival on 21 December to mark the winter solstice. There's a parade with bands and spectacular homemade lanterns (which of course ends in Madeira Drive), after which the lanterns are burnt on Brighton beach and a grand fireworks display lights up the sky over the English Channel.

• Pride

The highlight of the week-long summer Pride festival is the colourful parade. This one *starts* in Madeira Drive and takes a tortuous route to finish on the spreading lawns of Preston Park.

The beach

But at the end of the day – and, of course, during the day, too – it's the beach which gives Brighton its edge. It's been smartened up over the past few years, and there's plenty to do and see in the vicinity:

- The pier (it's free to enter)
- Nightclubs (mainly on the seafront and in West Street)
- Open-air concerts by Fatboy Slim and others
- Brighton Fishing Museum (under the arches – also free)
- Abstract beach sculptures (where else but in Brighton?)
- Swimming (but do wear beach shoes).

Have a great time!

Glossary

arable field A field for growing crops.

barrow A prehistoric burial mound.

bathing machine A shelter on wheels, which allowed bathers to descend into the sea in privacy.

cobbles Rounded stones or pebbles. Many older houses in Brighton have their exterior walls faced with cobbles, with bricks at the corners and around the doors and windows. The cobbles are traditionally painted black, the bricks white.

dhow A traditional Arab sailing ship.

dipper A person who helped bathers out of their bathing machines and thrust them into the water.

folly A building which is made purely for decoration and serves no useful purpose.

gaol The traditional British spelling of *jail*.

gasolier A light fitting similar to a chandelier, but powered by gas.

hogboat or **hoggie** A traditional Brighton fishing boat, now known only from pictures and models. It was unusually wide and had no keel so that it could easily be drawn up onto the beach.

laines The five large arable fields that surrounded the Old Town from medieval times until the 19th century. Each laine was divided into large sections called *furlongs*, and each furlong into narrow strips called *paul pieces*. Individuals might own or rent one or several paul pieces, which were not always next to one another. All the laines were built up in the 18th and 19th centuries, and only the North Laine is still referred to by its old name.

Lanes, The The area of small shops and narrow streets in the north-east corner of the Old Town. It was known in the 18th century as The Knab.

leakway A pathway between furlongs (*see under* laines).

mathematical tiles Overlapping clay tiles hung on the walls of a timber-framed building to give the appearance of bricks.

mausoleum A large, impressive tomb.

Mods Short for 'modernists', members of a teenage subculture in the 1950s and 60s who favoured handmade suits, pop music and motor scooters.

navvies Short for 'navigators', a term used for labourers who built canals in the 18th century and railways in the 19th.

Old Town The medieval part of Brighton, bounded by West, North and East Streets and the seafront.

palisade A strong fence made of wooden stakes or posts.

Pullman car A luxury railway carriage with restaurant facilities. Pullmans were invented in the USA, and introduced to Britain by the London, Brighton & South Coast Railway.

Rockers Members of a teenage subculture in the 1960s who favoured leather jackets, rock & roll music and motorbikes.

Roundheads A nickname for the short-haired soldiers of the Parliamentary Army during the English Civil War.

smallholder A person who owns or rents a small plot of land, usually just enough to grow food for their own family.

stucco A strong, long-lasting plaster used on outside walls.

Tractarian Movement (or Oxford Movement) A group within the Church of England whose elaborate rituals were sometimes criticised for being similar to those of the Roman Catholic Church.

twitten A local Sussex word for a narrow lane or passageway between buildings.

Timeline of Brighton history

c. 500,000 BC Boxgrove Man. Early Stone Age people use hand-axes to hunt bears, bison and rhinos.

c. 8000–4300 BC Mesolithic hunter-gatherers and hunter-fishers forage along the coast.

c. 4300–1500 BC New Stone Age people sink flint mines, and build a 'causewayed camp' on Whitehawk Hill.

c. 1500–700 BC Immigrant Bronze Age 'Beaker folk' construct burial mounds, including one near the sea at Hove which contains an amber cup.

c. 700 BC – AD 43 Celtic people smelt and forge iron, farm on lynchet (ridged and furrowed) fields and build defensive earthworks at Devil's Dyke and Hollingbury.

AD 43–410 Romans occupy Sussex, building a villa near Preston Park.

410 The Romans leave Celtic Britons to the mercy of invading Saxons.

681 St Wilfrid converts the Sussex people to Christianity.

1066 Norman invasion. Brighton is a small fishing village at this time.

1185 First mention of St Bartholomew's church (on the site of the present Town Hall).

1313 Brighton is granted a market charter.

1337–1453 Hundred Years' War between England and France.

1340 The sea swallows 16 hectares (40 acres) of farmland.

1349 The Black Death arrives in the Brighton area. Hangleton village is deserted.

1377 French pirates sack Rottingdean.

1497 A defensive bulwark is constructed on the coast.

1514 and **1545** The French burn Brighton.

1555 Brighton brewer Derrick Carver is burned at the stake in Lewes for his Protestant faith.

1558 A circular blockhouse is built on the seafront, with cannon mounted on the roof.

1580 Brighton has 80 fishing boats and a population of around 2,500.

1588 A beacon is lit to warn of the Spanish Armada, which passes the coast in late July.

1650 Brighton is the largest town in Sussex, while Hove is a row of cottages.

1651 The future King Charles II arrives disguised in Brighton and escapes to France in Nicholas Tettersell's coal brig.

1660 Charles II becomes King and Tettersell is rewarded with a pension for life. The modern name 'Brighton' is first used – among many other variations.

1665 A free school opens in the town.

1703 Brighton is badly damaged by a great storm.

1730 Great concern is expressed over the encroachment of the sea.

1739 Preston Manor is rebuilt by Thomas Weston.

1750 Dr Russell publishes his book advocating the sea-water cure.

1754 First bathing machines arrive.

1773 First theatre opens.

1783 The Prince of Wales pays his first visit to Brighton.

1785 The Prince secretly marries Maria Fitzherbert.

1789 A grammar school is opened.

1793 Two new gun batteries are built on the seafront.

1795 The Prince of Wales marries Caroline of Brunswick. Two soldiers are shot for mutiny at Goldstone Bottom.

1800 A pump room is built over the spring in St Ann's Well Gardens, Hove.

1811 The Prince of Wales becomes Regent because of his father's madness.

1815–1822 John Nash remodels Brighton Pavilion in oriental style.

1821 The Prince Regent is crowned King George IV. *Brighton Gazette, Sussex and General Advertiser* is first published.

1822 A continuous seafront thoroughfare, King's Road, is first opened.

1823 Opening of the Chain Pier.

1824 Steamships begin operating between Brighton and France. Arthur Wagner becomes vicar of Brighton (until 1870).

1825 The Royal German Spa opens in Queen's Park.

1831 Celia Holloway is murdered and buried at Lovers' Walk.

1833 The Anthaeum is erected in Palmeira Square – and collapses the day before its official opening.

1841 The London & Brighton Railway opens (later the London, Brighton & South Coast Railway). The town's population is now 47,000.

1844 Brighton's first chief constable, Henry Solomon, is murdered.

1848 Brighton College is founded.

1849 Cholera outbreak in Brighton.

1850 Brighton's Extra-Mural Cemetery is laid out. Henry Wagner is made perpetual curate of St Paul's church in West Street.

1859 Brighton Grammar School (now BHASVIC) founded.

1861 The Clayton Tunnel railway disaster kills 23 people and injures 176.

1864 Opening of the Grand Hotel.

1866 West Pier opens. Goldstone pumping station (now the British Engineerium) is built.

1867 The workhouse (later Brighton General Hospital) is built.

1872 Aquarium and Madeira Drive built.

1874 John Hawkshaw builds Brighton's intercepting sewer (a sewer that collects water from smaller sewers). Opening of Preston Park, Dome museum and library, and Booth Museum of Natural History.

1876 Brighton and Hove High School is founded in the former home of Thomas Read Kemp in Montpelier Road.

1881 Balcombe Tunnel murder.

1882 First telephone exchange is opened.

1883 Opening of Volk's Electric Railway.

1884 The 'Birdcage' Bandstand is erected on the seafront.

1885 The three Lawrence sisters found Roedean School.

1888 The Clock Tower is built.

1890 Hotel Metropole opens. Madeira Terrace extends from the Aquarium to Duke's Mound.

1896 The first film is shown in Brighton.

1899 The Palace Pier opens.

1901 The first trams run in Brighton.

1905 Preston Manor is enlarged.

1910 Opening of the Queen's Electric and Duke of York's cinemas.

1914–1918 First World War. The Royal Pavilion becomes a hospital for wounded Indian soldiers.

1921 The Chattri is unveiled on the Downs above Patcham and the South Gate of the Pavilion is dedicated. Both are memorials to Indian war dead.

1925 Boating pool built beyond the West Pier.

1928 Greater Brighton is created, and commemorated by the Pylons next to the A23.

1934 The Brighton trunk murders.

1939 Last trams and first trolleybuses run.

1939–1945 Second World War.

1940 Brighton beach is closed to the public. First air raid, 15 July. Odeon Cinema bombed, 14 September.

1943 Brighton's heaviest air raid, 25 May; 24 are killed and 51 seriously injured.

1961 University of Sussex founded. Last trolleybuses run.

1964 Mods and Rockers clash on Brighton seafront during the May Bank Holiday.

1966 Hove Town Hall burns down.

1968 Opening of Churchill Square shopping precinct.

1975 The West Pier closes.

1977 The Brighton Centre opens.

1979 Queen Elizabeth II opens Brighton Marina.

1980 Naturist beach opens.

1984 Grand Hotel is bombed by the IRA.

2000 Brighton and Hove is made a city.

2002 DJ Fatboy Slim organises the first of his beach parties, attracting a quarter of a million people to the seafront.

2003–2004 The wreck of the West Pier is set on fire twice.

2005 The award-winning Jubilee Library opens.

2007 The Royal Alexandra Hospital for sick children moves to a new site in the grounds of the Royal Sussex County Hospital.

2009 The Birdcage Bandstand is rebuilt.

Index

Other titles in
The Cherished Library

Ireland
A Very Peculiar History
With NO added Blarney
Jim Pipe

Scotland Vol. 1
A Very Peculiar History
With NO added Haggis
From ancient times to Robert the Bruce
Fiona Macdonald

Scotland Vol. 2
A Very Peculiar History
With NO added Bagpipes
From the Stewarts to modern Scotland
Fiona Macdonald

Heroes, Gods and Monsters of
Ancient Greek Mythology
Michael Ford

Heroes, Gods and Monsters of
Celtic Mythology
Fiona Macdonald

Brighton&Hove
NOT TRANSFERABLE

Brighton&Hove
NOT TRANSFERABLE

Route

2969   Ticke

Bus: 205

Daily: 37   Adult Si

Golds